W9-CQQ-738

Endorsements for

10 Discussions for **Effective Leadership**
10 Ways to Exceed your Expectations as a Leader

"The business world is in uncharted waters. The context has changed and new content must be created by releasing the creativity of "people." The Industrial Age leadership model of the past 100 years is "burned-out" yet it is the only way that many executives know how to lead. Ray and his colleagues have given an inspiring description of the new leadership principles. You must read, not to confirm the content you already know, rather contemplate how you would use the ten principles to create contextual clarity for your people. You can be a "different" leader tomorrow with this book as your guide."

—Thomas Wentz, President,
Corporate Performance Systems Inc.

"In my 35 plus years of studying, applying, writing about, and providing leadership development programs and services, I've come to the conclusion that there is a pressing need for a revolutionary new path for developing leaders at all levels. This book draws our attention to aspects of leadership that aim to do just that. As I work in my new project with Zenger-Folkman, I see the need to develop exceptional leaders that pay attention to these less conspicuous actions of effective leaders."

—Jim Clemmer,
Author of many books on leadership

10 Discussions
For
Effective
Leadership

PRO CHAT SERIES

10 Discussions For
Effective Leadership

10 Ways to Exceed Your Expectations as a Leader

By

Raymond Perras, Peak Performance Coach
Author of AïM for Life Mastery
with
Marcel Bellefeuille, Professional Sports Coach
Bruno Lindia, CEO, DMA Canada Ltd.

Cover design by Julie Bellefeuille

authorHOUSE®

AuthorHouse™
1663 Liberty Drive
Bloomington, IN 47403
www.authorhouse.com
Phone: 1-800-839-8640

© 2012 by Raymond Perras, Marcel Bellefeuille, Bruno Lindia. All rights reserved.

Cover Design by Julie Bellefeuille

Other books by Raymond Perras:
    AïM for Life Mastery – author
    Ready, Aim, Excel – contributor
    Ready, Aim, Captivate – contributor

No part of this book may be reproduced, stored in a retrieval system, or transmitted by any means without the written permission of the author.

Published by AuthorHouse   10/30/2012

ISBN: 978-1-4772-7770-6 (sc)
ISBN: 978-1-4772-7769-0 (hc)
ISBN: 978-1-4772-7768-3 (e)

Library of Congress Control Number: 2012918650

Any people depicted in stock imagery provided by Thinkstock are models, and such images are being used for illustrative purposes only.
Certain stock imagery © Thinkstock.

This book is printed on acid-free paper.

Because of the dynamic nature of the Internet, any web addresses or links contained in this book may have changed since publication and may no longer be valid. The views expressed in this work are solely those of the author and do not necessarily reflect the views of the publisher, and the publisher hereby disclaims any responsibility for them.

Dedication

To my brother Georges, who inspired me to seek continuous improvement by his honest and common sense philosophy toward the little things that make a big difference.

Raymond Perras

To Julie, Ymilie, Alexandra, Mathias and Cedrik, your sacrifices and unconditional love are truly a blessing. I love you with all my heart, soul and spirit.

Marcel Bellefeuille

To my life journey travel buddies, Lisa, Dominic and Matteo. Love forever!

Bruno Lindia

Contents

Foreword

As you read this book, you will discover the inner thoughts of three men who have consolidated their views on leadership actions that greatly influence the destiny of any organization or team. The lead writer is Raymond Perras, a peak performance coach in business and sports. His co-authors will bring two distinct real life perspectives throughout the book: Marcel Bellefeuille is a professional sports coach who will share the view from the sports angle; Bruno Lindia is a businessman who will look at leadership through the business lens.

We have different backgrounds but a common bond in wanting to help those who are tasked with the role of "leader" to act responsibly and with accountability.

Our aim is not to draft an all encompassing treatise. Instead, we want to share a floor level insight on the subject of leadership, the kind that creates an environment where people want to be, desire to work, and want to share experiences with fellow workers.

Even though we had a much longer list to start, we have chosen to focus on ten aspects or elements of leadership action that, in our collective experience, often are forgotten and end up undermining efforts and reducing expected results where teams are involved. We are sharing with you ten ways to become more effective as a leader.

You will read about leadership principles and practical experiences which will help define the context for your daily routine, a context that often seems invisible in your workplace. When you get to *About the Authors* at the end of the book, you will read about the source of our thinking on leadership; the chapter summarizes each of our individual path to the leadership table.

In this book, we have used the word "leader" to signify a person who has responsibility for a group or team in any organization. Remember that anyone can exercise leadership from any position in a hierarchy.

The goal of this book is to share insights with would-be or existing leaders. You have surely recognized the fragile equilibrium of your situation (the context). You are likely looking for some reference points (the content) that strengthen your conviction that your leadership actions have the potential for a high degree of success for your team.

As Tom Wentz[1] puts it, " . . . we must differentiate between context and content . . . . Most people read leadership books to merely "confirm" what they already KNOW. That does very little to actually change behavior." Our ten actions (or principles) are all about "effective behavior" change and that will not happen for the "content confirmation" reader.

Tom continues his reflection further: "The most effective books . . . are ones that serve as a "reference" to be

---

[1] Wentz, Thomas. Author and president, Corporate Performance Systems Inc.

"contemplated." That is what our 10 Discussions aim to be for the readers. This approach reinforces the format of discussing WITH the reader in order to point to "what could or should be done" to increase personal leadership effectiveness.

Another benefit we offer is to provide enough insight for you to decrease your fear of being seen as weak if you do not have all the answers, or sometimes need help to survive. It is acceptable to feel overwhelmed.

Many years ago, Max De Pree, former CEO of Herman Miller authored a book, *Leadership Jazz*[2]. De Pree pointed to a number of qualities to be an effective leader. The one that stuck with me was the ability to be vulnerable. As a leader, you don't need or want to be a superhero. You want to be perceived as an approachable person, one that leans on his team for sustained support, a person who respects his team members for who they are.

The reality is that we are all human beings struggling to create a good life for ourselves. Too often, we forget the little things, which usually turn out to make a big difference. Too often, we forget that people are the key to any successful endeavour. Too often, we forget that our teams are an ensemble of people, with diverse personalities and backgrounds, who are willing to compromise, collaborate and cooperate to produce synergy. Remembering those facts is the key to exceed expectations and release the human potential at play.

---

[2] De Pree, Max. *Leadership Jazz: The Essential Elements of a Great Leader*. 1st Edition by Doubleday. New York 1992. Revised Edition. Crown Business 2008.

10 Discussions for Effective Leadership

Success in an organization depends almost totally on a coming together of the minds. Sometimes, the leader gets overwhelmed by the context and commits the fatal mistake of perceiving people as machines, of forgetting that respect is a cornerstone enabler of performance. Absence of respect leads to reduced self-esteem, and self-esteem is the internal key to motivation and drive.

> *"In an age of large-scale events and organizations, the greatest single issue of importance, . . . is for the individual to feel that he counts."*
> **- Albert Einstein**

In such an environment, people soon feel like they don't count. Their ideas are not well-received or are outright relegated to the shelf for the sake of expediency. With time, a deep down feeling develops. People have a sense that it does not matter how much one tries, management will never be satisfied.

This feeling of not being part of the team or group is very real and is one of the most insidious issues of our time. Because everything is happening so fast, and technology has advanced by leaps and bounds, we have somewhat fallen behind in adapting to the speed of change. As long as our organizations treat people as human beings, the gap is bearable. But when overwhelmed by the demands of the organizational structures and policies, leaders will, at times, forget that they are dealing with human beings.

Another key concept in this book is the application of peak performance as a routine process to produce results. Peak performance is no mystery. It is the result of attention to the little things that make a big difference. Too often, people take a cursory look at little things and do not pay attention, assuming that we are all adults who can adjust, cope, and make the best of the situation.

In fact, when I wrote *AïM for Life Mastery*[3], my goal was to provide a simple approach to creating peak performance. I offered the following definition: **the right stuff, in the right amount, at the right time™**. It is not the pedal to the metal.

Rather, it is an awareness of what we carry as experience, knowledge and abilities used in the right measure at the most appropriate time. The end result is increased effectiveness with less effort or stress. It is to a great extent the ability to take care of the little things on a routine basis.

In the end, we are writing this book in the hope that we will help leaders create a better work environment for their teams. Leaders who read these pages and practice these leadership actions will likely integrate a new understanding. They will become more aware of how they can increase their ability to become truly effective leaders who routinely exceed their expectations.

Thank you for picking up the challenge and reading through our work. We hope it becomes a timely and helpful book on your path to productive and effective leadership.

---

[3] Perras, Raymond. *AïM for Life Mastery*. AuthorHouse. Indianapolis, 2011

The State of Leadership

(Setting the stage)

If we should forget that we are in the twenty-first century, it would be easy to commit the same sin of omission that often plagues those of us who do not learn from the past and forget to live in the present. The important thing to remember is that the present is where we prepare for the future.

When considering a set of reference points to enable effective, authentic and proactive leadership, it is useful to take a step back and take stock of where we have been and where we want to focus next.

There is enough knowledge and recognition to go around and smooth out the road for leadership candidates. However, as for so many other "soft skills", we lose sight of the important and the urgent as Stephen Covey[4] calls it, and get lost in the non-important and non-urgent details of everyday life. We get dragged around by the perceived urgent matters and forget that if we are to succeed, we must pay attention to the important stuff. When we talk about leadership, one aspect of the important stuff is the human factor.

---

[4] Covey, Stephen R. *The 7 Habits of Highly Effective People.* 15th Edition. Simon and Schuster Canada. Toronto 2004.

A Glance at the Past

In order to maintain perspective, it is useful to take a look back at the past. Leadership action in organizations has produced outstanding results in many instances, and poor results in others. Since it is said that up to 95 percent of humans are followers, it is obvious that leadership and the role of leaders has a significant impact on the outcomes in most domains.

In an effort to keep the focus on the more recent situations that surround us, we would like to use research conducted recently to illustrate the current context we operate in when it comes to leadership, and when seeking answers as to what our current and future leaders should be mindful about. We are referring here to recognized experts who have provided meaningful data that should sound an alarm for anyone concerned about the development of leaders in the 21st century.

When the consulting and training firm Development Dimensions International (DDI) released their *Global Leadership Forecast 2011*[5], it was billed as "the biggest study of its kind, involving over 2,600 organizations in 74 countries. Nearly 1,900 HR professionals and 12,500 leaders participated." It was the sixth biannual forecast they had completed since 1999.

Their conclusions pointed the way for every Human Resources (HR) department and executives willing to take

---

[5] Boatman, Jazmine Ph.D., and Wellins, Richard S., Ph.D. *Time for a Leadership Revolution*. Development Dimensions International. Pittsburg, USA 2011.

on the challenge of developing their leaders' skills. The goal would be to enable leaders to become more effective in their respective organizations. The report also provided a kind of roadmap for anyone already in a management role seeking to evaluate and continue to develop their own leadership skills.

Key findings of their research revealed some rather appalling numbers which confirmed what many people in the trenches say about the skills of their leaders:

Only 30% of leaders and 25% of HR respondents rated the quality of leadership in their organizations as very good or excellent.

The survey also attempted to pinpoint mission-critical skills that are required in the 21st century if an organization is to succeed. The five most important were (in rank order):
   1. Driving and managing change.
   2. Identifying and developing future talent.
   3. Fostering creativity and innovation.
   4. Coaching and developing others.
   5. Executing organizational strategy.

About half of the leaders surveyed rated themselves as ineffective in these five most critical skills.

> Note:
> We will attempt to provide some insights to reinforce the what and the how of these skills in the work place, and perhaps give you ideas on how to ensure effective action when we go through the 10 Discussions for Effective Leadership.

More Reflections;
It is not surprising that every one of these skills is aimed at the future. An organization must be forward looking (as opposed to blaming the past) if it is to adapt to the changing world we live in. Globalization has ensured that those who run on the spot are soon overtaken by everyone, even the ones who have lesser resources, talents, and knowledge.

In his new book, *The Future of Management*, author and professor Gary Hamel[6] comments on the backward nature of current organizations and emphasizes the need for rethinking leadership development to its core. His assessment hits hard at the systematic and structural limitations imposed by the old way. He says, "Right now, your company has 21st century, internet-enabled business processes, mid-20th century management processes, all built atop 19th century management principles."

This obvious disconnect has put at risk our ability to be effective leaders. A new awareness is required to ensure that all the various parts of a service or product delivery system work in unison to make optimal use of the human potential. That is the greatest challenge for today's leader.

Back to the DDI Forecast
In another section of the DDI report entitled "The role of management is still in yesteryear mode", DDI and Gary Hamel partnered to identify disablers in the workplace that act as natural barriers to effective leadership.

---

[6] Gary Hamel is the originator (with C.K. Prahalad) of the concept of core competencies in organizations.

In rank order, the following are identified as the top "Management Culture Killers". We have added comments at the end of each (**in bold**) to further clarify the situation according to our observations in most domains of workplace activity:

1. Strategic and key business decisions are made mostly by those in positions of power, with very few opportunities for open discussion. **In many organizations, it was found that "workers are asked to check their brains at the door".**

2. Organizational structure is based on silos, rigid, and hierarchal. **The poor soul who attempts to create cross-pollination of thinking may be at risk. If found out, retribution can go as far as being labeled a "trouble-maker".**

3. Management processes (e.g. strategic planning) are highly bureaucratic and often a nuisance. **More often than not, organizations fall into the trap that Warren Bennis[7] has termed "the effort to look good instead of doing good". Processes interfere with creative and effective work.**

4. Senior leaders are the primary visionaries and creators. **No effort is made to solicit ideas from those who do the work. For some reason, upper**

---

[7] Bennis, Warren. Organizational consultant and author of many books on leadership. Widely regarded as a pioneer of the contemporary field of Leadership Studies.

management has a tendency to think that the workers do not have the good of the company at heart. Yet, we have to ask the question, "Why do people come to work every morning?" Is it to do a BAD job? We don't believe that for one minute, and neither should you.

5. We almost exclusively focus on top/bottom line growth. **Human resources take a back seat, and are even shunned from the process for expediency, thereby forgetting that the bottom line is in great part due to the people who do the work. In fact, when the financial outlook becomes gloomy, human potential development is one of the first expenses to be eliminated.**

6. Power and influence are held by those who value the status quo. **Usually, there is minimal opportunity to think outside the box and implement creative thinking. "We've always done it that way" is the guiding refrain.**

These *Culture Killers* confirm the perceived insane approach of "doing the same old thing over and over, and expecting new results". As Hamel points out, it is critical that the approaches undergo major re-thinking if we are to remain effective, productive and efficient in the context of growing customized and client-centric service delivery. As Tom Wentz[8] points out, the old mass production system is "broken". We need to "create" solutions for the mass

---

[8] Wentz, Thomas. *Transformational Change. Going from Mass Production to Mass Customization.* Corporate Performance Systems Inc. 1999.

customization context if we are going to return to the dominant force North America was in the not too distant past.

Finally, as we often hear, "people don't quit a job; they quit their boss". That is the final nail in the coffin of leadership development as we know it. It is an outright condemnation of the level of leadership competence that is often found in many organizations. Perhaps you will be offended in reading this, but facts do not lie. The last piece of data from the DDI report we want to quote here is the degree of satisfaction of workers in general, as demonstrated by turnover and employee engagement.

DDI reports that when comparing companies by their financial successes, "there is a striking difference between the top third versus the bottom third performing companies". Companies that are recognized for authentic and proactive leadership outshine others by a wide margin.

These companies' human resources statistics are closely tied to their performance. Indeed, successful companies have 70% retention versus 24% for lower third performers.

Employee engagement is measured at 50% versus only 9%, and passion to lead is 53% versus a lowly 7% for the lower third performers! Is it any wonder that they are lower performers? People don't care, come to work only for a paycheque and the leadership transmits little enthusiasm for the organizational cause. Staff members are not engaged.

10 Discussions for Effective Leadership

Looking at the Challenges of the Future

We are heading straight into a leadership revolution. People are fed up with poor leadership. They want to come to work and enjoy their workplace and interact productively with their co-workers. They are seeking self-accomplishment, contribution, recognition and opportunities to grow.
More than anything, with human interaction raised to a high-fevered pitch by social media, people want to believe that they belong to the team or group with which they work or play. Again, that seems to be common sense.

But whether we have vilified the role of leader, or have lost the understanding of what motivates people, the DDI study raises some fundamental questions about where we are going. It is time to wake up and listen to the people who do the work.

Desirable Leadership Actions

A 2010 national survey developed for Public Works and Government Services Canada requested feedback on the role of leadership in the new work environment. People were asked to make suggestions as to what actions they would expect an ideal leader to take. The actions they listed do not necessarily mean that these are not taking place right now.

The list merely suggests a complete and total approach to leadership in the workplace when it comes to people responsible for a team. The results of the survey identified the following actions as highly desirable. They are not meant to be in order of importance. All are considered necessary to get the job done in a way that liberates the human potential in the group:

- Share the decision-making role
- Know how/when to communicate bad news
- Demonstrate equitability and fairness
- Speak the truth even if it is unpopular
- Partner in career planning for all staff
- Set the path to the goal, then step aside and allow people to get the work done
- Recognize/validate people's contributions
- Know, understand and apply evenly/consistently the company and organizational policies and rules
- Upgrade one's leadership skills regularly
- Create leadership think-tanks for best practices
- Support and groom the future leaders
- Practice empowerment by devolving responsibility and accountability
- Coach all staff in a timely manner
- Practice the "Give to get" process – respect and trust
- Be "hard" on the issues, "soft" on the people
- Encourage acceptance of diversity and set a positive example
- Explain upper-management decisions clearly
- Become a skilled communicator, fostering open and honest dialogue with staff.

Obviously, these actions do not reflect the statement that is made jokingly about some leaders. "It's my way or the highway".

Indeed, doing the same old thing will not bring new results. It is time to take a step back and rethink how we develop leaders. Perhaps more importantly, it is time to design how we are going to help those in positions of leadership to cope with the constantly changing context.

Tomorrow's leaders must be adept at promoting collaboration in creating or inventing our future. They must foster the development of strengths and competencies that fit the demands of the new globalized world. It is no longer sufficient to be a subject matter expert to be a leader.

In the new context, leaders must integrate alignment on organizational purpose as a key to supporting participative decision-making. Leaders must have the desire to put in place the training, the systems, the policies, the strategies, etc. (**capabilities**) that make maximum use of people's knowledge, skills and abilities (**competencies**) in a way that produces peak performance. Marrying the two leads to **effort-less effectiveness**[9].

At a glance, it becomes painfully obvious that leaders who have responsibility for a team or group have to be trained extensively beyond the conventionally accepted skills of the past. There are so many factors to deal with (just look back

---

[9] Effort-less effectiveness is a concept I developed in my book *AïM for Life Mastery*. It is the synergy of organizational capabilities and individual competencies, all aligned on purpose, that allow a team to minimize wasted time and energy and maximize results.

at the list of expectations) that you have to wonder who in his or her right mind wants to take on the challenge of leadership.

What Do We Do Now?

There is no doubt that the challenge is enormous. It can't be business as usual. The old way of doing things won't do. The leader of the future needs to develop an acute awareness of the fact that people are not machines.

I think that we still suffer from what I call the "Ford Syndrome". It used to be that what was manufactured was mass produced and that was what the consumer would buy. That also applied in the information business—like insurance—where a staff person dealt with one aspect of a policy application, then handed it off to the next officer who had responsibility for another part or aspect of the policy, and so on down the production line.

That assembly line concept has been completely demolished by the "mass customization approach" as Tom Wentz[10] calls it. Everyone wants a product to his or her specific requirements. Even in education, we have come to see people wanting to be selective in what their children are taught in school. Customization is a real concept which is gaining ground in our modern society.

Take a new car for instance. Features and options have become numbered in the hundreds. Gone are the days

---

[10] Wentz, Thomas. *Transformational Change. Going from Mass Production to Mass Customization.* Corporate Performance Systems Inc. 1999.

when one had to settle for whatever was produced. The same applies to information technology. Just think of Dell Computers who allow the buyer to build his or her own machine on the internet, picking from the hundreds of options, then on a push of a computer key, the order is sent to the floor and the computer is manufactured to specifications.

Let's not kid ourselves. This not only applies to manufactured goods. It also applies to a sports team where, for instance, over 40 individual players on a football team demand personal treatment.

Warren Bennis[11] is recognized as the authority on the subject of leadership. Many years ago, he advanced the concept that "an organization cannot be different from the person at the helm". There must be concordance between the leader's and the organization's values. In the 21st century, people now desire and act on their need for self-determination, self-satisfaction, recognition and contribution.

The new leader has to play with these dynamics. Otherwise, it takes little time before cracks appear in the organizational structure. Resources are wasted on the work required to either bring people in line with corporate thinking, or replenish the ranks due to the high turnover of personnel. As is often said, people don't quit a job, they quit a boss.

More and more, the practice of self-managed teams is becoming prevalent. The leader has to find the balance

---

[11] Bennis, Warren. *On Becoming a Leader*. 4th Edition. Basic Books. A member of Perseus Books. New York 2009.

between managing systems, policies, and administrative structures, and at the same time leading people on a worthy exercise to accomplish the company goals. That means establishing clear, understood and supported goals that make sense to the people.

Making sense does not necessarily mean abide by everyone's preference. Rather, it means upper management taking the time to explain the goals, listen to the people, and involve them in the decision-making process in order to create ownership.

On the surface, it seems that the leader's position has become a whole lot more complicated and difficult. But when we look more closely, if the practices espoused by Kouzes and Posner[12] are put to work, I submit that the work of a leader has become much easier (more on this in a later chapter).

The most obvious weight that has been lifted is that now, instead of one head and shoulders carrying the load, all members of the team carry a part of the load. The decision-making process takes a whole new twist as people take ownership of the direction that has been decided and participate in cooperative planning. Indeed, the leader's action is not to **PUSH**[13] anymore, but rather to guide the

---

[12] Kouzes, James M. and Posner, Barry Z. *The Leadership Challenge.* 4th Edition. Jossey-Bass. San Francisco 2007.
[13] PUSH refers to a concept of energy and effort applied to overcome natural barriers to performance while delivering results. It is centred on the leader.

PULL[14] of the group or team. That PULL provides a massive impetus to move toward the selected goals.

Given these observations, we have to conclude that leaders cannot be developed the same way they were in the past – pick the most knowledgeable person and put them at the head of the team.

Leaders now need to learn to be adaptable, flexible, vulnerable, attentive, aware of personal preferences, and ready to share the glory of success. In our brainstorming of critical factors that can make or break leaders, we came up with a long list of actions or aspects that require attention from a leader if she or he is to be successful. This book is not meant to be exhaustive. It only addresses some of the aspects of leadership considered necessary to forge alliances and create an environment where the optimal use of resources will ensure **effort-less effectiveness** – minimal efforts for maximum results.

An extensive study by the Zenger Folkman[15] Group provides further evidence that transforming the way we develop leaders is the key to the future success of any organization. Through extensive research across multiple domains and types of organizations, they report results that magnify the fundamental need to pay attention to the quality and the development strategies of our new leaders.

---

[14] PULL refers to the energy and drive generated by a team that understands the goal and commits as ONE to work toward that goal. In that instance, the role of the leader changes from "pusher" to "guide".

[15] Zenger, Dr. John H. and Folkman, Dr. Joseph R. *How To Be Exceptional: Drive Leadership Success by Magnifying Your Strengths.* McGraw-Hill, New York, 2012

They identify the following dramatic differences in organizational results for those with the strongest leaders:

- 3-5 times higher profits
- Up to 5 times higher sales revenues
- 2-3 times higher levels of employee engagement
- 3-4 times reduction in employees thinking about quitting
- 50% fewer employees that do leave
- Double the satisfaction with pay and job security
- 4-5 times more employees "willing to go the extra mile"
- 1.5 times higher customer satisfaction ratings
- Over 3 times safer work environment

As Jim Clemmer's *The Leader Letter* (September 2012)[16] puts it, "In a recent large scale global survey of CEOs and senior executives, 76 percent cited leadership development as important yet *only 7 (seven) percent* thought their organization was doing it effectively! No wonder we've got a leadership crisis!".

In light of these facts, as you read through the chapters, you will likely recognize situations where you could have been more effective. You may have read other leadership books and already have integrated some of the concepts that may be missing here. The fact is, in making the decision to share our leadership experience, we have aimed to provide a

---

[16] The article can be found at http://www.clemmergroup.com/webcast-zenger-folkman-s-extraordinary-strength-based-leadership-development-system.php.

compendium of activities that will surely help you find your appropriate pace as a leader.

We hope that for the less initiated and those who truly want to make a difference for their team, there is sufficient insight to assist you in building a stronger framework for your leadership actions.

We invite you to share our discussions for leadership effectiveness and find new ways to exceed your expectations wherever you may have taken on the role of leader.

The 10 Discussions

Understanding the Approach

> In an ideal world, everything would happen as it is supposed to. In reality, it seldom does.

(Ray setting the stage)

Even though there is a wealth of background material and knowledge available on leadership, more and more, the subject is recognized as a key element for organizational success that requires renewed focus. The reality is that we are not in an ideal world. And too often, things do not happen the way they should to ensure success in the field of leadership.

In our selection of "discussion" as a descriptor for our reflections, we have attempted to convey the sense that when talking about effective leadership, many stories can be told. And serious reflection is required to gain awareness of the things that can make a big difference in determining if you will be a successful leader.

Some stories are positive and inspiring. Others are remarkable by their striking resemblance to the "woulda, coulda, shoulda . . ." conclusion of things gone wrong.

In many instances, the stories allude to common sense approaches that ended up being "off the mark" actions leading to less than desirable results. The challenge was recognized and well-understood but unconscious neglect resulted in something less than acceptable. There was much talk but little action was taken to ensure success. What should have been did not pan out as expected when effective leadership is in action.

Therefore, the reflections we are offering for your consideration relate directly to elements of leadership that either propel a leader to success or interfere with the ability to achieve expected results. We think that it has become imperative to gain awareness of these leadership traps and strive to produce the inspiring type of results with which an effective leader empowers his team to act.

Arrangement of Each Chapter

The ten discussions are meant to raise your awareness of some critical facts or elements when faced with taking on a leadership role. In each chapter covering the 10 Discussions, we have provided a three-pronged approach to the exploration of each element. We aim to give you sequentially: 1) our general insight into leadership with respect to that element; 2) a sports perspective; and 3) a look through the business lens on how you may conceive a pathway to excellence in your leadership.

The first part of each chapter will provide insight into considerations associated with the leadership aspect being discussed. Whether it is the research of a well-known author, actual case studies by reputable organizations, or personal observations by the lead writer in his practice, the reader is provided with facts to set the stage for the item being discussed.

The second part of each chapter will focus on some observations/reflections by our professional sports co-author, giving a sports-based perspective to the action of leadership. It will look at the world of professional sports as seen through the eyes of a coach who takes this opportunity to show and elaborate on the realities of a domain that is a metaphor for life. People are involved, policies and practices are established, structures and plans are put in place, just like in any business venture. The difference is in the execution and the impacts of that execution. At times, contrary to business related interactions, the results are instantaneous and hard to manage.

The third part of each chapter will provide the business lens from our CEO co-author who deals with candidates and clients who seek to fill positions and jobs in a myriad of work domains, and the leadership opportunities and threats that appear daily in that context.

Each chapter will be closed with a summary or synthesis of the thoughts by the lead author.

Each of the two co-authors have shared (**with minimal editing**) their view of the work involved in being a leader, and provide some insights into what is important to remember in the daily routine. Stories will illustrate the seriousness and at times, the irony of the dynamics that make life as a leader a constant juggling act.

Our Invitation

You are invited to reflect on your own situation as you read through. Hopefully, you will recognize many instances of "déjà vu all over again" (Yogi Berra[17]) and realize that you are not alone. Hopefully, you will gain insight and ideas on how to tackle your leadership role in a more effective and efficient way.

The actions we will address were selected by a consensus vote amongst us based on our practical experiences in the workplace. Some may say that we have completely missed the boat. Others will feel like we are hitting the bull's-eye.

Others still will have mixed opinions about what we will advance.

In the end, it does not really matter. We are sure that everyone who reads the book will recognize situations or times where she or he has faced a similar challenge. You will relive the dilemma of whether to shut up and go away quietly, or rise and stand for common sense. You will remember how, if you were successful, you took action to make life as

---

[17] Berra, Yogi. Former major league baseball catcher and manager with the New York Yankees, well-known for his off the cuff quips.

enjoyable as possible for your team, no matter what decision was handed down by your upper management.

We firmly believe that the action of leadership is intertwined with personal interrelationships. Therefore, the discussions we are sharing will inevitably raise your awareness in other areas of leadership and help you become a more effective leader.

We have chosen these ten actions/elements of leadership and addressed them as realities that everyone lives with, is burdened by, or distracted from good work because they are not executed quite effectively. For those who succeed at these actions, you will conclude that you have what it takes to be an excellent leader.

For those who struggle, take heed of the pitfalls we have discussed. Maybe you can find some simple ideas to smooth out your road to leadership excellence.

Whatever you draw from this book in the way of insights or reminders, we invite you to integrate the new or renewed awareness in your own journey as a leader. If you think about your leadership actions using the lens of effectiveness, you will already have gained improvement since you will be working a little more on the process of being a leader. Your increased awareness will surely make you a better leader.

1 - The Right Stuff . . .

(prescription, dose, timeliness)

> *"If you choose peak performance, you will learn to apply the right stuff, in the right amount, at the right time."*
>
> **Raymond Perras,** author of *AïM for Life Mastery*

(Ray setting the stage)

In my book, *AïM for Life Mastery*[18], I provided an extensive explanation of my concept of peak performance, **the right stuff, in the right amount, at the right time™**. Peak performance is not the pedal to the metal. It is the acute awareness of whatever action or skill is needed in a certain circumstance, and the ability to apply the correct effort in a timely manner. All that happens in a way that reduces stress and increases focus so that minimal energy is expanded.

In the context of leadership as an action, the concept of peak performance is more applicable than ever. With everything going so fast and results expected "yesterday", it is essential that a leader learn to guide his team on a path of minimum effort to produce maximum results. That relates to the

---

[18] Perras, Raymond. *AïM for Life Mastery*. AuthorHouse. Indianapolis 2011.

appropriate knowledge or skill, in the right dosage and in a timely manner.

A leader cannot do it all to the extent that he or she provides the total PUSH. There must be a constant focus put on devolving responsibility and accountability to the team through a systematic and consistent framework so that the PULL comes from the team.

The aim must be to create an environment where people, everyone involved, take ownership and provide their own drive to create, sustain, and maintain momentum. This will usually produce the best results with the least effort. It becomes a collaborative and joint effort to minimize waste[19] in order to make optimal use of resources.

This calls for product or service delivery processes that are designed to fit the team's skills, competencies and expertise. These processes are understood, used across the board, and are respected and valued as the core structure of organizational success.

Unless everyone aligns on purpose and puts their competencies to the service of the common goal, there will be waste, and the team will be unable to produce at its maximum expected level.

Failing to minimize overlap, recycling, gaps in approaches and blind spots will inevitably result in unmet expectations

---

[19] The term "waste" is defined as the non-value-added work that usually results from lack of focus on being efficient and effective in the delivery process. It relates to the concept of total quality management (TQM) which was defined by W. Edwards Deming and addressed dead time and transport losses in any process.

and a lot of frustration for both management and the workers alike. Logically, a higher level of performance is expected when there are skills, knowledge and abilities applied to the various tasks. But that does not always happen when people are not aligned on purpose.

In spite of good will and desire, people who are involved will be disappointed or will disappoint their leader if he fails to explain his vision or organizational goals clearly – the right stuff. It will be difficult to make optimal use of their skills and knowledge. In some cases, it may result in the leader getting involved to do the work when he should have delegated the task.

This might happen for one of four reasons: 1) the leader lacks the trust necessary to let people operate on their own; 2) the people don't have the necessary guidance and training to get it done; 3) there is no clear vision to guide the team; or 4) the vision has been very poorly explained and is not understood by the team or workforce. In most cases, gaps in these areas result from failure to assign priorities, and the inability to recognize that some tasks deemed to be urgent are not so important in reality.

Basically, an effective leader will pay attention to **the right stuff, in the right amount, at the right time™** because it is the fast track to success. This approach enables the team to minimize waste and maximize results. Applying the concept is the foundation of a successful approach. Increased awareness of the benefits brings increased attention. Increased attention raises the potential for successful outcomes.

For example, the leader may request a report on a project without specifying the critical information he expects. The person assigned will do her best to review, assess and note the progress on the various fronts: installation, timing, resources spent, problems encountered, budget status, future challenges, potential issues for decisions, etc.

If in the leader's mind the goal was to produce a chart of the progress as compared to the initial plan, he may find what he needs in the report but it will take more effort. He will have to sift through the details. It will also have taken more effort for the person reporting because more information was generated than required. In the end, good work indeed, but not effective or efficient because "the right stuff" was not specified. And it resulted in a discrepancy between the "right amount" and what was expected. Timeliness would likely suffer and disappointment would likely surface on both sides.

Through the lack of regard for the right stuff, in the right amount, at the right time, much energy was spent which could have been saved. When resources are at a premium, it becomes obvious that attention to details and clear communication can make a big difference in the final outcome, at least from the point of view of good will and initiative.

Let's read about some real facts in the sports and business domains that demonstrate how a leader can easily fall in the trap and end up with unmet expectations.

^^^

The Sports Perspective *(Marcel)*

"Football is the ultimate team sport." I am sure most sports fans have heard this mantra. If that is so, then professional football is the ultimate organizational sport. The point is that although fans see the players and coaches perform on television each week, the preparation, performance and ultimate success of the teams is decided in many ways by a complete organizational effort. Professional sports are similar to the business world; it takes a complete organizational effort to have a successful product.

As I reflect on the theme of this chapter, it is important to put some structure to what I am going to discuss. So what is **"the right stuff, in the right amount, at the right time"** in football? For me, it can be stated as "**What you say, how much and when**".

What you say can take the form of a presentation, a trigger word or even something as subtle as a physical gesture. It is usually a response that is needed to refocus your team or an individual.

How much you say to your team mainly depends on the situation you are addressing. If you have ever heard the military term "conditional response", this definitely fits here.

Deciding when to intervene with some form of communication, correction or encouragement is always a critical decision. Specific situations need immediate feedback and others may require a more structured environment.

Let me share a few times when I was faced with some challenging decisions regarding this aspect of leadership.

This first situation is an example of a potential breakdown that could have ended our season on a sour note had it not been addressed in an appropriate fashion. Our football team was about to compete in a playoff game. This team had not had any post season success in many years. Everyone had worked extremely hard to bring the organization back to a place of respectability. Needless to say, post season success would help validate our efforts.

The night before we were to fly out for our game, we had to make a tough decision regarding our roster. It was decided that we would sit out one of our key players and leaders. Some unforeseen injuries had created a very difficult situation that required an equally difficult decision.

Obviously, the timing of these events was not ideal. The leaders on our team had expressed some concern. They were not sure that our younger players would understand the situation and this might upset the psyche of the team.

That night I pondered; how should I deal with this situation? There were those around me that felt nothing needed to be said. They felt a coach's decision is just that. However, I have always believed that if there is a **"moose on the table"** you better discuss how it got there. So, I set out to inject **the right stuff, in the right amount, at the right time**.

I decided that the right time to discuss the issue and remove the moose would be at our team meeting the next morning prior to leaving for our road trip. It was critical to avoid disturbing the team chemistry in a time of such pressure.

The right stuff was to emphasize that all the players, even ones not making the trip were very important to our success. As a head coach, it is necessary to make every player on the team feel that their contributions are a valuable part of the process of winning. Furthermore, I decided to discuss this specific player's situation in order to remove any doubt about the reasons for our decision.

It was critical to frame it as a one game scenario and not something that would be a factor beyond that. It was also important to communicate that our decision was based on the best potential for the team, not on that player's performance.

That morning I addressed the situation in front of the team. We talked about the player's value to the team and what would be needed to replace him. I openly asked certain players to step up and fill the void created by his absence. Each of them committed to contribute more in different areas to honour the team and their teammate. This situation could really have had a negative effect on us. However, our team came together as a result of our openness and desire to do the right thing – communicate in a timely and clear fashion. All the credit goes to our players for rallying together for the common purpose.

We won the playoff game and the player was re-inserted in the line-up for our next game. Crisis averted.

In some situations, less is more. The second example I want to share is a time when I was a head coach at the collegiate level. It was the night before the "National Championship" game. We had a team meeting in the ballroom of a prestigious hotel. I had arranged for a guest speaker to address the team. As the players began to arrive, a group of them entered the room in slippers wearing the hotel robes from the rooms.

My first thought was to aggressively address the situation. They were not dressed appropriately, and our program would have to pay for these robes if damaged or not returned (all considerations when coaching amateur sport).

As I walked to the back of the room, they knew I was going to deal with this deviation from our team principles. Then it occurred to me, perhaps they were just letting off some nervous steam. This team had never played in such a big game. So I set out to inject **the right stuff, in the right amount, at the right time**.

As I approached them, I said "gentlemen, where are your smoking pipes?" We all had a chuckle and I started the meeting. It was just enough to break the tension and set the mood to be at peak performance.

In the same vein, you can also derail your team's efforts when you deliver "**the wrong stuff, in the wrong amount, at the wrong time**".

I recall breaking my golden rule prior to an important game. Never break the momentum of your preparation close to competition.

Our team had a terrible practice the last day prior to an important game. After practice I was less than complimentary to our players. They knew how angry and disappointed I was with our execution that day.

The problem when you push buttons closer to competition is that you do not always have enough time to bring your people back to a place of confidence. Furthermore, it was just a handful of key people that upset the execution of our practice. I should not have addressed the whole team regarding it. I am sure half of them wondered what I was talking about. Needless to say, we did not play as well as we could have in that game. The key players who practised below our standards also played the game that way. The old adage "You play as you practice" surely applied here.

Leaders cannot always be the ones pushing the buttons. It is important that you give your team the opportunity to recognize their mistakes and correct themselves. Continually lashing out may alienate you from your team and render you ineffective as a leader.

The challenge occurs when you do not have enough people on your team or in your organization that are prepared to make others around them accountable for their quality of preparation. That is what I qualify as "not having the right people on the bus".

"The wrong stuff, in the wrong amount, at the wrong time" can also come from any area in your organization. That is especially true when senior management is not on **"the same page"** as the team leader.

As a coach, I have seen teams in many different sports underachieve when different messages are sent from other areas of the organization.

It can happen directly, or through the media. Sometimes a coach may decide to downplay the importance of an upcoming game to relieve some pressure from his athletes. The choice is to focus only on the process during that week. However, conflicting messages outside the direct chain of command could affect the performance of the team. Players may press, or work outside their abilities and job responsibilities if they have the sense that there may be underlying consequences if they fail. In these cases, all leaders in an organization have to trust their people to get the job done.

So the question you have to answer is: "How do you ultimately achieve **effort-less effectiveness**?"

One mission-critical aspect is that everyone in the organization must share the same vision, and formulate the messages in the same sense. Every member of the team has to pay attention to **the right stuff, in the right amount, at the right time**. Otherwise, the organization, as viewed from the outside or even from different internal departments, can appear disjointed and misaligned on the common goals.

Whether you are a manager or a head coach, there is always someone above you in a team or organizational structure. There has to be a common vision that is developed and shared from top to bottom. One cannot be naïve enough to believe they can be successful at the highest level if the whole organization is not on the same page. A childlike faith can only carry you so far.

^^

The Business Lens *(Bruno)*

> *"Hard" Task + Process = Simpler*

The right stuff, in the right amount, at the right time: simple to say, simple to understand but almost impossible to implement; impossible if there is no structure around the words.

With respect to the right stuff, let's consider this. When assessing any task, people tend to rank it on a scale of difficulty. "Easy" to "Hard".

When I first started REALLY working on Peak Performance concepts, it occurred to me that I would say that things were "Easy" or "Hard". I then noticed that I wasn't the only one. This is fine if it is in a simple conversation with a friend, but in a more serious exchange this may present a challenge with meeting the other person's perceived expectation.

After further reflection and dialogue with professionals, the conclusion was that nothing in the world is "Easy". Without the proper framework, "easy" can become a "Hard" thing. And that is where the right stuff comes into play. Having a clear approach to the issue can help to apply the right stuff.

For example, someone used "Breathing" as "Easy". However, if you have Asthma, it is very "Hard". Another person said "Walking" was "Easy". But it is not so for someone who is in a wheelchair.

So do we conclude that everything is "Hard"?

Consider this. A new task may have a high degree of complexity. It may require years of technical training to get good at it. The tradesperson goes about performing the task and he makes it seem effortless. In reality, a great tradesperson has developed habits that allow it to appear "Easy". We are simply observing the process that has been established through repetition and now appears to be "Simple". The right stuff enables the tradesperson to make it look easy. In other words, nothing is "Easy", but developing and aiming to perfect a process to allow the execution of the task will make it "Simpler".

My equation is now: **"Hard" Task + Process = Simpler.**

Although this may seem very obvious when we are dealing with high performance, definition is of paramount importance. Of course, as "simpler" takes root, it becomes easier to apply the right amount. The effort can be measured and minimized so that the process is efficient and produces the desired result.

In business, the two rarest commodities are Money and Time. Without money you have no time and if you waste time you will have no money.

Superior use of time is the complete opposite of wasting time. Again, I am stating the obvious. However, think of all the time that is wasted on trying to understand what the other person meant when they said this is "easy" and should take but a few minutes. How many times have we heard "do you have a quick minute to spare?"

In reality there is no such thing as a "quick minute". Every minute has sixty seconds and most of these interruptions take more than 60 seconds to complete. Actually, when someone asks for a quick minute, it not only takes you away from your present task for several minutes, but it will take you several more minutes and sometimes hours or days to get back to your original state.

I like to use the term "timely". The term "timely" triggers my mind to be aware that it may or may not be the right time to do or say something. Timing is everything.

Think of a funny comedian. The delivery of the material at the right time makes the comedian funny. We have all encountered the comment: "the joke is funnier when my brother tells it". Chances are the brother's timing is better.

In sales training, an exercise that has proven to be effective has been "The yellow submarine" exercise. It goes like this:

We write down the words of the chorus of the popular Beatles song "Yellow Submarine". Each sales person is asked to sing it out loud the way they have heard it sung by the Beatles. What we notice is that although we have heard the song several times, each salesperson sings it in a slightly different tone, rhythm and tempo. The song then doesn't sound the same.

We then ask the trainees to sing it together but putting different time value to each syllable. This further distorts the song. The simple point I am making is that when delivering a sales presentation, it is important to be completely aware of Tonality, Tempo and Rhythm. This comes with practice. A lot of practice! Most people try to "Wing it". This is a sure formula for disaster.

Having a clear idea delivered at the right tempo, in a timely fashion and containing the right content requires mastery of the **Right Stuff – Right Amount – Right Time.**

Another example of the right stuff in the right amount at the right time is when a manager is upset about a missed deliverable and plans to confront the employee(s). The unprepared manager ends up going too hard on the person(s). He often forgets the peak performance concept and makes the mistake of thinking that the employee needs a tongue lashing. Often, the employee feels just as upset as the manager does about the miscue.

Considering when to say it and how it should be said is equally as important as what is said. Careful planning leads to a clear understanding of what is the best solution going forward. The employee(s) and manager are equally vested in the project. There is often a mistaken belief that one party has more to lose than the other. That usually tilts the sense of the message and results in perceived inequality or unfair decisions.

> **"We are all good people just aiming for different things."**

Remember! Everyone is born with pride and a strong willingness to succeed. We should recognize that we are all good people just aiming for different things. Sometimes, compromise goes a long way in ensuring team harmony.

With proper planning and a strong awareness of the Right Stuff – Right Amount – Right Time principle, you will be able to understand and appreciate the other person's goals and expectations. This will create clarity and certainty within your organization.

Believe it or not, this is attained by simply spending a few minutes a day discussing and sharing that vision with someone. In very large organizations, it is impossible to see and talk with everyone every day. However, it is important that when you do have an opportunity, as brief as it is, you take a few seconds to say something positive in line with the corporate vision. It will be greatly appreciated.

Having been involved in the human resource business for most of my life, this proves to be difficult at times. I am not suggesting that this comes quickly. People change on a minute to minute basis. But, so do you and I. This is the beauty and not the challenge of dealing with people. If you understand this fundamental rule, you will be better prepared for any situation that may come up.

Setting and communicating expectations relative to the overall goal is essential for a successful result. In the end, you get what you set.

Once you become aware of the necessary balance between the Right Stuff – Right Amount – Right Time and how it relates to your overall goal, you will find it simpler to have effective dialogues with employees, clients and prospects.

Keep the concept in mind. Going all out all the time can be a dangerous approach. You may set yourself up to eventually crash and burn. Be aware of when you need to accelerate, decelerate and sometimes even to completely STOP.

∧∧∧∧∧∧∧∧∧∧∧∧∧∧∧∧∧∧∧∧∧∧∧∧∧∧∧∧∧∧∧∧∧∧∧∧∧

Concluding Remarks (Ray)

Aiming for peak performance, **the right stuff, in the right amount, at the right time™** is simpler than you may think. It requires awareness and common sense. And it is based on recognizing each and everyone's potential, the task at hand, and the other resources available. Mix that with the involvement of those who are part of the team and you have a solid recipe for success.

The following reality is inescapable. Nowadays, we are asked to do more with less. The truth is, there is no way to do more with less, only the ability to do less with less. Unless you become painfully aware of this fact, you run the chance of running yourself and your team to the ground. With time, no one will have the strength and the focus to do the best possible job.

When you read the above comments, I am sure you have already detected the sense of urgency that accompanies this message of **the right stuff, in the right amount, at the right time™**.

We live in a globalized free market economy and the sooner we get familiar with what it entails, the sooner we will be able to put our effort to the task of becoming highly performing organizations. This resides totally on the shoulders of the leadership who have the responsibility to lead the way. As a leader, you now have to find ways to unburden your team, remove barriers to performance, and facilitate the full deployment of your team members' capabilities.

It is undeniable that the goal should be to minimize waste and maximize results. Past experiences usually provide a good reference point on what to do and what not to do.

Take time to step back. Strive to use the peak performance recipe, **the right stuff, in the right amount, at the right**

time™. Be a model leader: involve those you are responsible for, charge them with creating collective intelligence[20], and shoot for effort-less effectiveness. Make sure awareness is the foundation of your leadership excellence.

You will sow the seeds of excellence and you will soon feel the PULL. It is not too late! Start now! Make sure to use **the right stuff, in the right amount, at the right time™.**

Using the peak performance formula will take you closer to the application of another leadership action which usually produces optimal results. We are aiming here at empowerment of the team members. However, a leader has to become clear on what empowerment entails, otherwise, the word empowerment will be a myth in the workplace.

In our next discussion, let's consider how a leader can avoid the myth of empowerment.

---

[20] Collective intelligence is a concept I learned working with Tom Wentz, author of the book *Transformational Change.* It refers to the ability of a group to build a composite of the local knowledge and expertise that includes the thinking of all the people who are involved and aligned on a common purpose. It usually produces the optimal result.

2 - The Myth of Empowerment

(lots of talk, not much walk)

> *"The more credit you give away, the more will come back to you. The more you help others, the more they will want to help you".*
> **- Brian Tracy**, self-help author and motivational speaker

(Ray setting the stage)

As Brian Tracy says, a fundamental principle always at work in an organization of any kind is "what you give is what you get". Empowerment respects this principle and it is a sad place where leaders forget or neglect to apply it.

The following are a few reflections that we hope will raise your awareness of the fact that the power and capability of your team is a direct result of your ability to allow them to take charge. It takes courage and faith but the rewards are endless.

Many years ago, William C. Byham, Ph.D.[21] with co-author Jeff Cox laid out the four cornerstones of empowerment. As a book review put it, their book provides " . . . specific strategies designed to help you encourage responsibility, acknowledgment, and creativity so that employees feel they **own** their jobs." It was the result of research conducted in over 400 companies to define how people can be empowered, and how leaders should act in order to achieve empowerment, an action that is now recognized to be a key element of success in organizations.

Their title revealed the essence of the conclusion they had found. The deal was, you can either *Zapp* your people or *Sapp* them. You can empower them or you can render them helpless.

Byham summarized the concept at work in the four cornerstones of empowerment:

- Maintain self-esteem; remind people of their past performance and ability to get it done;
- Listen to understand how a person feels; find the motivation that makes people go beyond the call of duty, and then,
- Ask for their help in getting things done; involve them in the HOW; give them freedom to perform to the top of their ability, and
- Offer help (when required) without taking responsibility.

---

[21] Byham, William C. and Cox, Jeff. *Zapp! The Lightning of Empowerment*. Ballantine Books. Revised Edition. New York. 1998.

When we look at these actions, it seems common sense all the way. Yet, how many people in positions of leadership forget these simple approaches that *Zapp* people? They go on their merry way, walking around, talking on the phone, sending emails, tweeting even, in ways that *Sapp* people.

For most people who have to endure these behaviours, life can be miserable. No wonder that organizations that allow their leaders to *Sapp* the workforce struggle at times to produce expected results. Usually, that is reflected on the bottom line.

We are sure that in your experience, you have felt the energy-dousing effect of sapping comments just like you have had the wonderful experience of being zapped by a leader who, by knowledge or accident, touched you with a bolt of empowerment.

The fact of the matter is that empowerment is a much travelled concept which is often misunderstood and not properly applied.

Depending on the perspective, it takes different shapes. One that focuses on the "-power-" part of the word was admirably discussed by Diane Tracy[22], founder and CEO of her consulting firm Tracy Communications Inc. Tracy explains that in her view, people are given power through 10 clearly defined steps – the Power Pyramid. The sides of the pyramid contain the three elements (or steps) that make devolving power possible: **trust, respect and permission to**

---

[22] Tracy, Diane. *10 Steps to Empowerment: A common-sense Guide to Managing People.* William Morrow and Company. New York 1990.

fail. Everyone looking to empower others should remember those three enabling steps.

The word empowerment has also been integrated into training and other personal development efforts. However, we will often hear that empowerment is a myth. It is talked about, paraded as a belief, lauded as a desirable behaviour, wanted by those who do the work, but often disregarded when the time comes for a leader to act.

Either leaders just give lip service and keep the reins tight because they don't trust their people, or they just plain don't know how to *Zapp* their people by implementing the four cornerstones of empowerment.

Just like a chair or piece of furniture, empowerment will be solid only when the four legs (cornerstones) are set strongly in place. Bottom line, you need the four actions if empowerment is to be effective. A missing leg creates a teetering situation which topples over when things get stressful. Then, it is much more difficult to recover. At that time, people realize that indeed, empowerment was a myth.

For today's and tomorrow's leaders, it is mission-critical that they learn to empower their people, *Zapp* them into a liberated state of performance. Every organization can and will benefit immensely from applying the lightning bolt of empowerment.

Further insight into ways and means to empower people can be gained by reading Peter Jensen[23] on how a leader

---

[23] Jensen, Dr Peter. *Igniting the 3rd Factor*. Performance Coaching Inc. 2008.

can fire up his charges. Jensen states that a leader has the responsibility to: 1) manage oneself; 2) build trust with the team; 3) use imagery (vision) to help people see the bright future; 4) uncover and work through barriers and obstacles to performance; and 5) welcome adversity as an opportunity to learn and grow.

It is not rocket science, just common sense which sometimes is forgotten. When things are not going well in the team, a leader would do well to step back and observe what he or she is doing, or not doing, that leads to less than expected results. People come to work to do a good job. Leaders should learn to empower them to do so.

Let's now read reflections from both a sport perspective and a business lens. Perhaps you will be reminded of instances in your daily routine where Zapping or Sapping occurred.

^^^

The Sports Perspective *(Marcel)*

The myth of empowerment in professional sports is as real as the drama that unfolds on the field each week. In this section, I had to ask myself the question, "What is the myth?" When talking to players and coaches, many different aspects of empowerment come to mind. It means a lot of different things to different people. First, let's talk about the myth as it exists in professional football.

Empowerment does not really happen at the professional football level. It is an excellent abstract word that gets people excited to join an organization. There are even moments of empowerment where a person believes that he is given the authority and the responsibility to execute a project. But in the end, true empowerment cannot exist if every decision is questioned at some point in time.

The reality is that we work within a larger framework. Accountability to top management is beyond what most professions demand. Professional players and coaches are evaluated on a weekly basis and are subsequently hired and fired based on those results. Here today and gone tomorrow certainly applies to our profession. Furthermore, the success of the team is a direct result of each member being able to contribute with a high level of discipline and unselfishness. Many times, that only happens because of the dedication of the people involved to their sport, and not because they are empowered.

The ability of each individual in a professional sports organization is often dependant on someone else being effective in their own position. As I stated earlier, this also includes leaders and managers who are not part of the competition each week. This level of dependence on each other contradicts the whole concept of empowerment. If that is not enough, the speed at which our industry works demands constant supervision and checkpoints.

Throughout my career, I have had the opportunity to be part of the hiring process at many levels. There are a number of themes that consistently recur when the topic of empowerment is raised.

Decision Making

People want to make decisions that relate to their position. In reality, they want the freedom to set the direction in the area that they work. This often relates to the specific expertise of the person in that position and their individual philosophy. Unfortunately, it has to fit a much larger context. If you have an offensive coordinator that is intent on implementing a system that does not fit the skill sets of the players, the head coach has to intervene. The direction of that area of your team has to be monitored, not allowing for complete autonomy. If not, many people will be held responsible for a lack of results.

How often have you heard a coach state that a player has made a bad decision on the field? Usually they are talking about a play that ends up in an error.

There are times when this happens because a player has not followed his base read or missed an assignment. Players and coaches always want to do the right things. Sometimes decisions are made outside the framework of what is to be implemented. When people make decisions independently in our sport, they are exercising the freedom that is desired. Unfortunately, if you are wrong, there is a high cost to pay.

As you can see, giving people complete freedom to do as they see fit in our industry has dire consequences. It can be very challenging for your team to meet this type of expectation. The level of consistency in the decision making process requires constant reminders and follow up.

Working Independently Does Not Work

Most people want to do their job with minimal to no interference. "Let me do my job" is probably the number one request from people in most professions. It certainly is in professional sports. Football is the ultimate team sport. This factor is diametrically opposed to the concept of working independently.

Professional football has evaluation processes unlike any other business. Everything you do on a daily basis is evaluated. If you are a player, it means that you are critiqued on everything you do and say each day. Grades are given and feedback is immediate. Coaches are evaluated with every play, practice plan and response they give daily to the media. Again, feedback is immediate from management. Furthermore, the constant pressure and reminders are also reiterated from fans daily. The social media age in which we live only reinforces these realities.

With the exception of upper management, it is impossible to work with minimal interference in this or any other environment. It is impossible to work independently.

The by-product of this type of evaluation process is that adjustment and changes are happening daily, many times at the request of direct supervisors or upper management. It is this sense of urgency that demands that the speed at which recommendations are made does not always provide for collaboration and gradual influence.

Allowing people to fail

Most people expect some allowances for mistakes in the workplace. They acknowledge that mistakes will be made when given the opportunity to work in an empowered state. This certainly provides an opportunity for personal growth. While each different industry allows for some margin of error while maintaining reasonable levels of success, professional sports has very little room for error.

Football is a game that requires multiple players playing in unison at any given moment. Each player has a specific responsibility during each play that demands knowledge and physical execution. We are referring to execution of assignments that have little room for error.

Consider the numbers. If each player was making two mistakes per game, 22-24 players (22—US game, 24—Canadian game) are on the field during a play, and an approximate total of 60-65 plays occur on each side of the ball (120-130 total), there could easily be mistakes in around 40-45% of the plays in a game. Now factor in mistakes from coaches and you might *have a 45-50% ratio of errors to plays. No business could survive if this were your average.*

These numbers are nowhere near the reality in our business. Perhaps this is why it is such a structured environment. True empowerment and acceptance in high performance industries that are very dependent on teamwork create many challenges. Checks and balances are put in place to limit mistakes. Games are won and lost by four or five plays in most instances. Jobs can also be lost on a few crucial errors in judgment.

Now the good news!

There can be levels of true empowerment in every workplace. As I just discussed, we must first put away the myth of complete empowerment. It is much better to enter every situation with brutal honesty and clear cut expectations that may create opportunities for empowerment.

The challenge is "How do we create an environment where our employees feel empowered, in spite of the realities of the workplace? How do we maintain self-esteem and create opportunities for our people to have autonomy?"

One way I believe it can happen is that the organization must have a clear and defined vision that is initiated at the top and resonates throughout the organization. I was once told that it is difficult at times to have the senior managers on the same page at the same time. Well, it may explain why some teams succeed and others fail. Once a common vision is in place and accepted, there must be a defined set of processes that will ensure all members of the organization are proceeding in the same direction.

For most managers, it is difficult to put a proper structure to these statements. But this is mission-critical! No plan in any organization is valuable unless it is consistently executed at every level. However, if you can put this structure in place, you will have created an environment that includes and promotes empowerment.

When members of a team know exactly what and how the organizational goals are set, they are more likely to make the right decisions. They will need less supervision to complete tasks that are in line with the operational plan. They will make fewer errors. They will seek more input and be open to critique of their work beyond what would be expected.

I have been through many rebuilding projects as a coach. They all start with a vision. In one case, management had a clear and defined vision of the type of team we were going to become and how to achieve this objective. We were going to build a team with great speed and athleticism. This team was going to have many players with diverse skill sets and be interchangeable. The team was going to be built with youth, both at the coaching and player level. This would allow the core members to mature together, learn, and have experiences that would strengthen the entire team for the future.

Having established the what, we could now delve into the how. The selection process would be defined by the required skill sets. There would be a major focus on the fundamentals necessary to improve overall team abilities. Teaching methods and skill development had to relate to the age and experience level of our recruits. Systems and schemes also had to be developed to allow for individuals with different learning curves.

The clear vision effectively empowered the staff. Scouts had a concise idea of what style of player was necessary to fit this philosophy. Their decisions and recommendations were almost always in line with what was required. Little time had to be spent meeting or redirecting their approach. Coaches would create schemes that fit the knowledge and skill base of these players. They had the ability to work independently and made few errors executing this plan.

Players worked on their individual skill development and film review to shorten the learning curve. People in the organization searched for feedback and opportunities to be critiqued. Regardless of the scrutiny of the system's checks and balances, we felt empowered.

When decisions were being considered beyond the organizational objectives, there was a review process to allow input from those involved so that we ensured everyone was on the same page. Everyone had the opportunity to think outside the box. There were opportunities to present arguments when we felt that decisions did not fit our vision. These discussions were held before any permanent decision was finalized.

The guardrails that kept us on course were quite simple. As we moved along in our daily tasks we could encourage and re-direct each other with a simple question. Does this decision, action or behaviour align with organizational objectives? It was a great way to challenge each other in a non-confrontational way.

However, there are consequences for that style of incremental growth. The process took longer to show results. Fans and supporters had to be patient. There would be times of uncertainty, but the rewards were great. There would be long term success that was sustainable. The key to the approach was the resolve demonstrated by upper management. The ability to stay the course and repel the criticisms and pressures was critical. The long term effect of this foundation was a period of success that spanned eight seasons and two management regimes.

In this way, I believe we were all empowered to lead!

After sharing these past experiences, I hope that you can relate to your own career and recognize when you were empowered. If you note times when that was not the case, it is now time to plan a course of action to ensure that, now that you are a leader, you are truly a source of empowerment for your team.

^^

The Business Lens (*Bruno*)

Empowerment is one of the most overused but least implemented words in the business universe.

> **Behave it. Don't say it!**

For me when it comes to the word Empowerment. "Behave it" and "Don't say it".

This is almost like the game of charades where you know the word or phrase but you need to act it out without using words.

In order to have an empowered team, the groundwork needs to be in place so that people can make judicious choices aligned to a common goal. In reality, they are making decisions that are in line with a stated purpose (vision). Once clear expectations are set relative to the organizational vision (goals), decisions can be made with more certainty.

"Empowerment" in business, can be related to parenting. Responsible parenting leads to Empowered children. "The child who is allowed to become independent and self sufficient no longer relies on the parent". That defines a successful relationship between parent and child. This also applies to our team members and employees. But then, what is our worth if they no longer need us?

When I became a parent, I learned about a few things that I should be mindful of and to which I should pay attention.

The main one was that it is really easy being a father but impossibly difficult being a parent. The tough part is when you realize that your children have become a "mini" you. At an early age they pick up every word, every move and every bad habit you have by simply observing and imitating you. By the way, the same is true for a leader in any organization.

You quickly learn to watch what you say and do in front of children. Most of us insist our children try their best, be the best, listen, work hard, reach for the stars etc. but do we follow our own advice? It is so simple to say it but quite difficult to do it.

The key notion from parenting is that once we develop and implement positive habits, it is more likely that the child will pick up these habits.

The same applies in the business world. If you want your employees or clients to behave in an ethical and professional way, start behaving in an ethical and professional manner. It is the surest way to empower them.

Amazingly, if you *"Walk-it",* others will walk alongside you.

Believe it or not, most everyone wants to be associated with successful, motivated and ethical people.

It takes time and awareness to empower employees. It doesn't happen overnight. Staff cannot be empowered without first having a dialogue around goals, expectations and expertise. You may mean " . . . go ahead . . . try it and let me know how it goes", but in the end, you better be clear.

During interviews, I have fun when I hear the candidate say that they want to work for a company that "empowers" their employees. The fun starts when I ask: "What does that mean to you?".

Many are surprised by that question because empowerment has become synonymous with good management practices. Again without proper definition, it is but another word that means something to one and another thing to someone else.

The answers I get back are often:
"Not to be Micro-managed"
"Tell me what needs to be done and leave me alone"
"Let me make my own decisions"
Let us examine these answers.

"Not being micro-managed"
When I question people who answer this way, it becomes clear that there have not been any clear expectations set. I believe that both the manager and the employee need to

clearly define what needs to be done, when it needs to be delivered and how it needs to be delivered.

My next question becomes: "What steps have **you** taken to ensure that realistic work expectations have been set?" This usually gets the person thinking that they are part of the solution.

Micro-management is generally used to describe a negative experience. It is sometimes related to the leader's insecurity around the deliverables and the methods to deliver.

The insecurity can be generated by either technical or management incompetence. This is not to say that the leaders are incompetent, rather that they lack the particular capacity to effectively lead the initiative. This insecurity most often results in overly aggressive inspection of tasks delegated to people who know what they are doing.

"Tell me what needs to be done and leave me alone." This is a classic example of an answer received from someone who needs to be told what to do! If you are looking for a collaborative type, this person may not be the right fit. Although there is a time and place for independent work, this is not a characteristic of an empowered person.

The simple statement "Tell me" suggests that the employee does not know where to start! Conversely, a person who demonstrates clarity of vision will entice a leader to empower such people because they inspire hope in their own way.

"Leave me alone" is a hint that people are not interested in collaborating with others. You can work with these people but beware of the balance of "time and money". In every situation, there is an optimum point where you reach a diminishing return for the resources you apply.

"Let me make my own decisions."
In an empowered environment, decisions can be made both independently and in groups. I believe that what the person means to say is "what decisions can I make without consulting you?"

The only way a person can make all the decisions independently is when he or she owns the company. Even at that, great company leaders and owners will not make all the decisions on their own.

If you are willing to take *all* the responsibility for the outcome then you can make all the decisions. With freedom comes great responsibility.

In a prudent company setting, the risk is reduced if other major stakeholders are made aware of the policy options being considered and offer strategic advice.
Those are three examples of empowerment options.
One thing to remember is that we need to be clear that empowerment is an *action and not just a word*.

It suggests a *behaviour* that confirms to the staff that we work together and that clear expectations have been set. Trust has been established and we have the same benefits to gain or lose from each other's actions.

We have an ongoing joke at the office, when a University summer student comes in to work for us. We ask what type of environment they excel in. If they answer an empowered one, we look at each other and answer something like:"Great to hear . . . We empower you to make the coffee in the morning, wash the floors in the afternoon and clean the coffee pot at night . . . . great to have you on board!"

They usually don't find this very funny, but soon learn to not take it too seriously.

We go on to explain: "Let's work together for a bit. We'll see how we meet expectations, make decisions, handle freedom, work with others, exceed goals, and empowerment will take care of itself."

ΛΛΛΛΛΛΛΛΛΛΛΛΛΛΛΛΛΛΛΛΛΛΛΛΛΛΛΛΛΛΛΛΛΛΛΛ

Concluding Remarks (*Ray*)

We are constantly being reminded of the need for leaders to empower staff. But do we really know and understand what this implies? Do we realize that empowerment is a sustained and continuous effort to enable people to act?

Whether it is through direct delegation and a true accountability framework or explicitly providing a clear explanation of how a leader views empowerment, there is always room for interpretation. The key is to be consistent and stay focused on the end goal, holding true to integrity, and acting in a way that is aligned with your beliefs and values.

When everything has been said and done, the reality of empowerment always points to four leadership actions:

- practice your ability to help maintain self-esteem for the person you are coaching and leading;
- strive to understand how that person feels so that you know his or her source of motivation;
- ask for help to demonstrate vulnerability in specific and timely moments; and,
- offer help without withdrawing the delegated responsibility, so that your people can render true accountability.

Taking such actions will lead to the rewards of true empowerment: responsible, accountable and reliable people who make achievement of your goals so much easier.

As Diane Tracy explained, the leader should enable people to become empowered through the focused application of trust, respect and permission to fail. This is a tall order for a leader when failure is seen as negative instead of an "opportunity to start over with new knowledge" as Henry Ford saw it. It takes courage and strength of character to allow results to potentially be less than expected.

Practicing empowerment soon reduces mistakes and failures because it allows people to gain confidence in their abilities and competency to take on the task. It also allows people to develop the courage to ask for help (leading by example) when they are not sure of their capability to execute. That propels people to greater excellence.

I would assume that, as a leader, seeing your team members take initiative and PULL instead of waiting to be pushed is definitely a secret desire which you wake up with every day. Take action, empower your people, and reap the rewards!

Your gains in empowerment will be mitigated if you forget to trust your team members and become too involved in producing results. Balance is the key word to guide your effort, and trust will help you stay in balance.

Let's have a look at one action that may make or break your efforts to be an effective leader – the ability to trust.

3 - Trust and the Boomerang Theory

(a mission-critical action)

> *"We're never so vulnerable than when we trust someone - but paradoxically, if we cannot trust, neither can we find love or joy."*
> **- Walter Anderson,** author (The Confidence Course) and editor of *Parade* magazine.

(Ray setting the stage)

When I go into organizations as a performance coach, I ask people what is the one thing they would change if they had a magic wand. Inevitably, the answer points to lack of trust from management.

People do not generally feel trusted by management. Even if they come in every day and give one hundred percent effort, there is a sense that management is not satisfied; it is not enough. Do you think that these people want to be loved? Maybe, but one thing is for sure, they would like to be trusted.

What makes them think that? Well, for one, critical information is not shared, at least in a timely fashion. People find out from external sources, or after the critical moment has passed. How can they respond and act in a timely fashion?

Another indicator is the fact that people are not asked for their opinion on important matters. Very often, they are informed about decisions that affect them once the strategy and plans have been put in place. In some instances, they are not given clear direction on the common goals. Other times, they only get sketchy information.

In other instances, management does not listen to staff when problems are identified, defined, assessed and even provided with options for solutions. Upper management does not use their suggestions, and does not explain the reasons.

What can be more frustrating than to witness poor or disastrous outcomes when it would have been preventable had management considered the information and knowledge presented by their staff?

In these instances or other lesser moments, the perceived distrust undermines people's will to perform at a high level of excellence. Yet many organizations benefit from the integrity of their people in spite of management's signals of distrust.

Trust like many other aspects of workplace dynamics is an element that can be built over time. What I have observed and gathered over the years is that trust must be built on a solid foundation, and that foundation starts with the leader behaving in a way that demonstrates trustworthiness.

The leader will usually build trust with his team by gaining credibility. It is the foundation for imparting trust to everyone.

And credibility is created by four core actions which every effective leader takes great care to live and demonstrate on a continuous basis:

- Integrity lived through congruence, acting in line with beliefs and values, no matter what the circumstance.

- Intent which is explained, clarified and shared in a personal agenda. There is no doubt for anyone involved about what the leader wants to accomplish, or wants the team to do.

- Capabilities demonstrated by decisions which lead to positive outcomes, and actions that add value to the efforts of the team.

- Predictable results reflecting the leader's steadiness in addressing issues and challenges. People appreciate the predictability of the actions that lead to success. They admire the track record.

Trust will be built by giving reason to the staff for trusting their leader. These actions are an outward expression of trust that motivates team members to reciprocate: collaboration engenders cooperation. That is how trust respects the Boomerang Theory[24].

Indeed, how can a person expect to be trusted if he/she is not ready to trust in the first place? People usually respond

---

[24] This is a concept I developed many years ago while delivering workshops on leadership, team building and teamwork. Trust is one of the elements of team building that provides the glue to hold the parts together. When trust is given freely, it usually comes back like a boomerang.

to expectations we bestow on them. And people will be moved to trust if the expression of trust of their leader is open and forthcoming. Thus, this concept of trust can be equated to a boomerang. When it is thrown well, it comes back to the one who threw it. Learn to trust and you will benefit from the Boomerang Theory.

Here is another perspective on the value of trust and how it complements the foundation of an effective organization.

A lack of trust in organizational dynamics results in a dysfunctional team. Is it not what you have observed?

Trust either creates a nearly indestructible foundation for a team, or quickly allows it to disintegrate, no matter

> *"To be trusted is a greater compliment than to be loved."*
> - **George MacDonald**

what the members might attempt in trying to maintain its integrity. This is a powerful yet deceptively simple message for all those who strive to be exceptional team leaders. It is more beneficial to seek to be trusted than to want to be loved. Put another way, it is better to want to be respected than to be admired.

To be an effective leader who empowers people, trust must be a key ingredient of how you act every day moving forward. And for those who take heed, trust is one of those blessings that must be earned by giving it first. Trust respects the Boomerang Theory. You get it back if you throw it out first then act consistently to make sure it comes back to you.

Now let us see how the concept applies in sports and business, as discussed by our co-authors.

∧∧

The Sports Perspective *(Marcel)*

The issue of trust is one that runs deep through every area of our lives. It encompasses our personal relationships, professional endeavours and spiritual journeys. As we move forward talking about trust in sport, it is important to define the different levels of trust. I like to look at trust as it relates to our personal and professional lives. Most people would agree that the level of trust we expect and desire in our personal lives is much higher than that in our professional lives.

Have you ever heard "I would trust my life with that person"? We are almost always talking about a spouse, parent, sibling or lifelong friend. It is rarely with respect to a co-worker, unless a longstanding friendship has developed outside of the office. If you feel this way about your co-workers or teammates, you are destined for great things.

Personal trust

How many of us would simply hand over our car keys to a new neighbour if they asked? Have you ever loaned money to someone that you barely knew? How about leaving your children with strangers? The answer to these questions is obvious. There are personal situations that require a level of trust that is earned through time and experience together.

Professional Trust

Now, let us consider this approach from a professional point of view. If you are the owner of a locksmith company, would you send a recently hired locksmith on a call to repair someone's front door?

In another example, you are the chief financial officer for the company. You have just recently hired someone to do the company's payroll. Do you trust them to do it? The answer to these questions is obvious. They were hired to do these jobs. The difference is you are relying on their ability and competence to do the job (assuming their reference check was reliable). You trust them implicitly. They did not have to earn your trust in order for you to believe they would do what is required.

The Boomerang Theory

The "Boomerang Theory" simply means, if you give trust freely, it will come back to you. When you throw a boomerang with the right technique, it comes back to you. The challenge with this thinking is that it contradicts everything we have been taught. From a young age, you are taught that trust is earned.

In order to be successful professionally, it is of the utmost importance to give trust freely. The boomerang has to be thrown out to your team in incremental fashion, progressively further and further. When it is not, the organization may be limited in building a solid foundation for trust.

One definition of trust is "the quality of a person in whom we place confidence". Usually, we place our trust in people who are hired because of their expertise. I know, it is much easier said than done. As a football coach, I have been on both sides of the fence. I have been relentless in pursuing trust and yet not giving it. I have had the trust of those above me and been in situations when trust has been withheld from me. These experiences have shaped my views on this issue.

Trust as confidence

The concept of the boomerang has many examples in the game of football and the business of football. There are many examples demonstrated on the field. One area of trust that you see each week is the connection between quarterbacks and wide receivers. The best thrown passes are the ones where the receiver has his back to the quarterback when the ball is released. They allow the receiver to be more effective in deceiving his defender. The ball is thrown in anticipation of the receiver breaking into a specific area. The quarterback has to trust that the receiver will break into that area at a specific time. If not, the ball will be intercepted or incomplete. Often, these are plays that can change the outcome of a game.

If the quarterback does not trust, he is likely to hold on to the ball longer and get sacked. If he trusts that the receiver will do as expected, he will likely be successful. It is a game of decision in a fraction of a second.

So what leads to the trust factor between players? In some instances, it is the time the players have worked together: how often they have attempted that specific play; the experience level of the players; the confidence that the coaches have in the players to call that play; the previous successes; the low risk associated with that play. These are all factors that players have to take into consideration before making decisions that happen in the blink of an eye.

If we accept "The boomerang theory", the throw should be made all the time. It is the only way the team can be successful (assuming there is an open window in the defence); both quarterback and receiver trust each other to execute. The theory of given trust allows for success much sooner because it dictates a more aggressive approach to playing the game.

Trust as a discipline

Over my career, I have sat in many meetings and heard players and coaches repeat "Do your job". The most successful teams have coaches and players that have a "narrow focus". They only worry about the things that they can control. The challenge is that it takes great discipline to trust the man next to you.

I can recall doing a film review after a game; we had watched our opponent making a run for a big gain. One of our defensive linemen had left his position to make a play. When he was questioned about it, he responded, "I did not think my teammate would be in his gap (area of responsibility)". When I asked him if he trusted his teammate, he replied with an emphatic "Yes".

The runner had reversed his field and come back to his area which resulted in a big play. His teammate had temporarily been out of position but recovered in time. Unfortunately, the lineman being questioned overran the play because he had attempted to do both his and the other player's job.

This is a typical situation. Teammates trust each other, but something they see in the blink of an eye, alters their decisions. I call it "losing trust discipline". We try to do someone else's job because we feel in that instance that they will not get the job done. We lose trust temporarily because of an outside influence.

Giving trust freely and maintaining the discipline to allow people to grow is a difficult practice. Furthermore, it is a natural human instinct to believe that we can do something better than others. People that rise to leadership positions do so partially because they have been successful filling the role of the people they now manage. Because of their past experience, such leaders are very confident people and will have a tendency to trust themselves more than others.

These are all factors that make it naturally difficult to give trust before it is earned. The challenge is that when we do not give trust freely, we unintentionally risk undermining the efforts of the team.

Walk the Talk
When the boomerang is thrown with proper technique it will come back. The key to this statement is "with proper technique". Throughout this book you will hear the mantra "walk the talk". Our ability as leaders to "walk the talk" in every area of leadership is always being tested.

I am sure most of you have worked for someone who claimed to trust you implicitly. They hired you because they believed you could do the job. Then they turn around and micro-manage all of your efforts. Perhaps it was second guessing some of your decisions. Most people have worked for someone who has treated them in that fashion. Our natural instinct as humans is to withhold trust from that person.

It is important to continue giving trust freely if you want to receive it. Regardless of how you have been treated, if you are in a position of leadership, you can decide to lead your staff and employees in a way that helps them become trustworthy. Remember, the best teams and organizations have people who focus on what they can control.

In football, there are many layers of leadership in the hierarchy. Many people have the opportunity to practice the "boomerang theory". As a Head Coach, I have had the opportunity to practice this with assistant coaches, players and support staff. So what is the right technique? How do you walk the talk? Simply put, if you have the opportunity to give trust freely, follow through.

For example, when you ask for input, implement some of their ideas. When meeting with coaches, I have the opportunity to ask for feedback. When they ask me to make an adjustment, it is important that I follow through and make the adjustment. If I trust them enough to ask for their input, it is important to walk the talk and implement their ideas.

Consider the other side of the coin. When assistants are asked for input and it is not acted upon, the staff members will feel that they are not trusted. The enquiries are not seen as sincere, regardless of the intent. You will probably hear remarks such as "why even ask?" These are normal reactions from people when their input is not taken into consideration. This is especially true of situations that directly affect their jobs.

There was a time when I hired a young coach, and had a challenging time finding the balance between helping and micro-managing him. He did an excellent job from week to week and handled the situation very well. I suspect that although I threw out the boomerang, I did not always use the right technique. Fortunately, he always handled the situation professionally and responded with respect.

That was a situation where my leadership demanded that I intervene and take charge. I had to ensure his lack of experience did not result in omissions. It demonstrated how important it is that you know the difference between the need to intervene, and not giving trust freely to your people.

When the Boomerang Comes Back

When the boomerang comes back, it is a very powerful tool. The level of trust you receive from your people is confirmed by their actions. Buy-in does not have to be sought. Decisions can be made without lengthy explanations. People around you will trust that you have a good reason for your decisions. There will be no water cooler discussions after meetings. Daily activities will be executed without drama. When times of adversity hit, people will meet your expectations.

There is another advantage to giving trust to the people in your organization before it is earned. Naturally, you will be inclined to think the best of everyone. Your first instinct in times of uncertainty will be positive. Your tendency to develop false perceptions will be reduced. You will seek to know the facts before jumping to conclusions. As a young coach, I saved myself a lot of embarrassment by practising this leadership technique.

There have been times over my career when players or coaches have had personal misfortunes that have caused them to fail in meeting organizational goals. My first concern has always been for their personal well-being. This has helped me to take the time to find out why they could not meet expectations, and I avoided misjudging them. It resulted in long term positive outcomes and increased trust between us. It pays to trust people without waiting for them to trust you.

Obviously, success and failure hinge on many different factors and people in every organization. Giving trust is but one facet of leadership. It does not stand alone. But, if you do not strive to trust freely, you may find yourself standing alone.

So go ahead, throw the boomerang out there! Don't be surprised to see it come back.

^^

The Business Lens (*Bruno*)

If you want to be trusted, you need to trust others first. And the first person you need to feel comfortable trusting is "YOURSELF". How can you expect something that you can't expect from yourself?

> **"Trust in order to be Trusted"**

We are all human and have weaknesses and strengths. It is acceptable to recognize your vulnerability and say, "I don't know", "I am not sure", "I am not an expert". Staff will figure it out anyways. Once you are aware of your limitations and are able to communicate it to others without fear, you can trust yourself and others will trust you too.

For example, I had an exceptional person that worked with our firm for a few years. He was a great contributor especially during the demanding company start-up period. I honestly could not have asked for a more loyal and productive person.

The plan was that he would eventually become a partner of the company. The progressive plan was in place and we were both enthusiastically working on it. He was younger than I. I was quite excited that, some day, he might want to own and run the company. He took ownership for the company results and people gravitated toward him. He was viewed as and WAS a leader.

At the time, it was a great situation.

Then, the economy started to turn and a few personal issues came up and it seemed like he was unsure about the future. All that had a significant impact on him. He tried to hide it but I noticed a few things, mainly hesitation to commit.

We chatted about his concerns and he said that it was nothing. We were very polite and professional about our business and personal relationship. Others in the company also noticed the ever so slight change. Another colleague asked why I was being so patient with him and his non-commitment behaviour. Great question! Why was I delaying successful implementation of the plan? Why was

I not making a decision? People started thinking that the person was the problem.

I then figured out that the problem was that *I could not trust myself* in this situation. This went on for about a month. Our business moves so quickly that in a month we probably discussed the issue a few times. When we approached the subject, we did not really deal with it because of the respect we had for each other and our commitment to our clients and consultants.

Once I realized that I could not trust myself in dealing directly with his non-commitment, I told the person that I would engage a professional facilitator to help us resolve the issue. He agreed, and I hired Ray.

We then set up a phone conference where the person and I were in my office and Ray was in his office 2000 miles away. Ray started by asking a few targeted questions to clarify the situation. It did not take long before the person scribbled something on a piece of paper while Ray was talking. It read: "this is very difficult for me . . . . It must be difficult for you . . . I am sorry . . . I know what I need to do . . . . Thank you . . ."

The call was planned for 90 minutes with a few more follow up calls scheduled for the next few weeks. I politely interrupted Ray and advised that we had come to a resolution.

Ray asked what the conclusion was. The person said: "I will resign and move on". It was a very sad day. He was very mature about it and we have not only remained good friends but he has become a client of our firm.

Who knows how it would have turned out had I not figured out that I could not trust myself in that situation? Sometime, even with the best of intention, a leader can be the master of his own demise.

Let us look at another angle of leadership. The greatest thing about being involved as a leader and coach in business and sport is that when facilitating a session, you are surrounded by incredibly talented, intelligent and creative people. I listen and learn so much from the people in the room.

When I witness productive and effective discussions by these smart people, I use the term "zip words" as a way of consolidating the ideas, perspectives and meanings of a word to create a memorable concept. Zipping is tremendously useful when we encounter similar situations. It allows us to get on the same page in a flash.

For example, we may want to anchor the word respect as a key part of our delivery framework at DMA. The team will brainstorm ideas and angles on how the term is reflected in our daily routine, and with our clients and associates. Then, we consolidate those reflections into a few bullet sentences and give it a "zip word". We may chose a sign or a word to put it all together – e.g., a smile, a jolly hello, or a written note bearing the word "respect". The key is to use a trigger to remind each other of that part of our common mission.

It is the same concept of a "zip file" that brings data together in a smaller format. We find it useful in reminding ourselves of the agreements or commitments we made as a team.

This is the same thing as a quarterback on the playing field who uses a wristband with a few words on it. The "zipped words" are the keys to remembering a much larger play book. The important thing here is to appreciate the time, effort and practice that goes into "zipping" words that way.

For me, "Trust" is one such "zipped" word that ALWAYS comes up in team sessions. Everyone agrees that you need trust to be an effective team. I start by asking the individuals what that word means to them. The "UNzipping" then begins.

In my years of coaching and running my business, this is how I have "zipped" the word TRUST into five distinct aspects of leadership.

> **T-** *Tell the truth*
> **R-** *Respect*
> **U-** *Unity*
> **S-** *Support*
> **T-** *Together*

T—Tell the truth

As the leader or owner of your company, when you communicate the truth about your intentions and motives, others will tell you the truth. If they do not reciprocate, you may want to reconsider your relationship with that person.

Ask pertinent questions so that you fully understand what is to be expected and then truthfully state if you can live up to those expectations.

Telling the truth is easier than lying. The truth eliminates speculation and installs certainty. Human beings thrive in an environment of certainty. People know what is coming. Remember to apply "the Right stuff, in the right amount , at the right time" when telling the truth.

R—Respect
Respect is an *action* word. It emphasizes self-awareness and awareness of others sharing the same planet. We are all born equally and have the right to happiness and success. That is the fundamental of Respect. We are all good people aiming for different things. Again you absolutely need to respect yourself first. Apply the golden rule: treat others as you would like them to treat you.

U—Unity
This is the ability to bring the goals into one vision. If this is accomplished, all parties will see the benefit of the relationship moving forward. It can only be achieved with effective dialogue that aligns everyone on the organizational goals. All for one, and one for all must be the byword in the daily routine.

S—Support
This is the feeling and belief that you are on the same team and someone has your back in difficult times. Be mindful of others. They may need you in the most unexpected moment. Always remember that we should not be going at it alone if we are to succeed as a team.

T—Together

This is best described by something that my sons started saying at an early age when we asked them to clean up the play room: ***"let's work together so we don't work forever"***

Teamwork builds trust. Working together toward the common goal is one of the best ways to demonstrate and give trust.

In summary, paying attention to these elements of trust will usually bring you much closer to success in all your endeavours. Stay focused and make sure that trust is the key word in your day.

∧∧∧∧∧∧∧∧∧∧∧∧∧∧∧∧∧∧∧∧∧∧∧∧∧∧∧∧∧∧∧∧∧∧∧∧∧

Concluding Remarks (Ray)

As you read through the preceding reflections, you probably remembered instances where you either created trust through sending the boomerang the correct way, or at other times, wondered what you had done to create a lack of trust.

However, if you are looking for a quick set up to enhance your efforts and effectiveness as a leader, the above provides sufficient insight to enable you to take action and install trust in your environment and workplace.

The key is to respect the need for people to be trusted in order to entice them to trust you. Marcel pointed out that what we mean here is trust for those you have enrolled to be part of your team. Strangers may not deserve blind trust, but your people do. It is a prescription for success. The reason is simple. When you trust people, they trust you, and then barriers between plans and execution are removed.

> *"The leaders who work most effectively, it seems to me, never say I. And that's not because they have trained themselves not to say I. They don't think I. They think **we**; they think **team**. They understand their job is to make the team function. They accept responsibility and don't sidestep it, but **WE** gets the credit. This is what creates trust, what enables you to get the task done."*
> **- Peter Drucker,** legendary author and management guru.

As Drucker points out, the leaders will do well if they learn to use the word "we" in any dialogue with their teams. Using the "we" implicitly transfers the notion of trust. As Bruno pointed out, doing so demonstrates the trust for the people and helps them to build a solid foundation from where to trust. And giving credit to the "we" seals the deal and encourages the team members to take initiative because they feel trusted.

Remember Bruno's acronym:
T – tell the truth
R – respect others
U – unity of goal achievement
S – support each other on the drive to achieve
T – together; "Let's work together so we don't work forever".

As trust is a fundamental element of leadership, one that either makes or breaks your ability to lead, make sure you keep it in mind and position it as one of the mission-critical behaviours that will increase your potential for success.

Learn to throw the boomerang. You will only get what you give. It is a law of nature. I am sure that deep down, you desire to be trusted. So, go out and send trust, and it will come back to you.

The application of this fundamental principle will be much easier if you take the time and commit to the practice of our next discussion . . . telling the truth.

4 - Telling The Truth

(beware holding back some facts, or twisting it . . .)

> *"You can bend it and twist it .... You can misuse and abuse it ... But even God cannot change the Truth."*
>
> - **Michael Levy**, international radio host, mystical poet, business and finance philosopher.

(Ray setting the stage)

As we pointed out at the beginning, these discussions are not in order of importance. Notionally, they are all important, and perhaps could be labeled as all mission-critical for a leader to succeed.

Telling the truth is definitely a mission-critical aspect of the leader's responsibilities. More often than not, this element of leadership will greatly impact your team members either positively or negatively. The challenge for the leader is to know how to tell the truth so that the team will respond in a constructive manner.

Unfortunately, there are times when the truth (message from upper management) coming down is sure to hurt the troops. Now the leader has a crucial dilemma. Tell it like it is, or try to reduce the impact by withholding some information, or twisting it to avoid demoralizing the people?

In our experience, the hard truth hurts, but in the long run, people appreciate having the leader speak the truth. Sometime, as leaders, we are too compassionate, not trusting the ability of our people to deal with less than expected promises or decisions. Of course, the truth will be devastating if it is uncovered for what it is; a semi-truth or an outright lie.

In an ideal situation, where people are trusted and seen as responsible adults who have ownership of the current situation, the truth will just be another challenge which the team can take on enthusiastically.

Together, the sense is that nothing can defeat us. We have confidence in our ability and skills to overcome. We trust that each member on the team has our back. No one will allow us to flounder, crumble under the weight of the obstacle the truth brings on, or fail outright at meeting expectations.

The key is to know <u>how</u> and <u>when</u> to share the truth, and do it even if it hurts. In the long run, knowing who you are as a leader, what you are, and accepting this will serve well in telling the truth in all circumstances – short term pain for long term gain.

As a leader, you may at times have to make some tough decisions; to tell or not to tell the truth.

The following are two perspectives on telling the truth which give the different insights from our co-authors. Be sure to reflect on your own experience as they share context and circumstances where they have been faced with that leadership challenge.

∧∧∧

The Sports Perspective *(Marcel)*

Telling the truth, sounds simple, but it may be one of the toughest things to do. The reason for this is because it will make you feel uncomfortable. Remember, reaching out of the usual boundary is the only way to grow.

These feelings will be a result of saying and doing things that will cause you to look at yourself and be brutally honest with those around you. I always believed that real change can only occur from confrontation, whether that is confronting oneself or others. Confrontations can also bring forward other underlying issues that you may have overlooked. Once the door is open, people will usually put forth all the things that are frustrating them. These are excellent opportunities to uncover issues that could possibly derail your organizational efforts.

Be honest with yourself

With respect to football and leadership issues, I have always tried to practice looking at myself first. "The buck stops here" is my way of looking at this. First, it is often very constructive to look at yourself and recognize your mistakes or shortcomings. I want to make sure I tell myself the truth. This is called initiating personal growth.

The challenge is that growth can only happen if you are willing to be brutally honest with yourself. A technique that I like to use is to pretend that in all instances, I applied the correct approach and used the necessary facts in choosing what actions I would take. Then I step back and assess the decisions that had a negative outcome.

As a coach, you hire assistants and decide who the starting players are. These decisions are often based on different sets of criteria. They are often done in collaboration with the staff and management. They are always done with the utmost consideration for the evaluation processes we have put in place.

One would therefore expect that the best possible decisions would always be made. However, from time to time, you may find that a particular coach or player may not be the right person for the vision and direction of your team. These people can easily take your team off its course to success.

When that happens, it is the most helpless feeling any leader can have. You may feel let down and angry with these types of people. The key is to stay objective and find a way to keep everyone on track in spite of the disruption. Your discussions will revolve around these individuals and how they affected the team's level of success. In these moments, it is critical to tell the truth, no matter how much it hurts.

When I have found myself in these situations, I used my evaluation technique to find the source of these mistaken choices, and ultimately, I had to point the finger at myself.

Mind you, there are always "red flags" that surround these decisions. Sometimes we put blinders on for different reasons and hope for the best.

In such situations, I have always learned and grown in my ability to weigh the facts and make tough decisions. Being brutally honest with myself has allowed me to implement a new filter when assessing future members of any team.

I have learned that if we place fault only at the feet of others, we forsake the opportunity to grow and make changes in our approach. In the end, making the effort to grow personally at every opportunity will protect your efforts in the future.

In a nutshell, you have to learn to tell yourself the truth before being able to tell the truth to others. The questions are, "How and when to be honest with the people you manage? What is the best timing? What is the best environment?"

Principles for Telling the Truth
In sports as in business, the key elements of success are the people who do the work. For me, telling the truth has roots in some generic principles that I want to share with you, especially with respect to my area of expertise, football.

A)   **Feedback needs to be immediate** – It is always important to give feedback at the appropriate time. In football, we will always make the correction as it happens, again in film review and finally in a grade format. It may seem like overkill, but people need to know what they did wrong and how to fix it. I have never encountered a player or coach that did not want to do it right!

B)   **Be brutally honest** – There cannot be growth without telling the truth. I have often had to evaluate myself or others and needed to be honest with the evaluations. If I told a player his footwork was adequate, he probably would not work on it. The reality is that adequate is not good enough to be successful. I should tell him that he needs to improve in that area and seek to be excellent since it is a fundamental skill for his play execution.

C)   **Be specific** – When you talk to a group or individual, give them specific examples of what and who you are talking about. Address specific units of your team if you are giving instruction or sharing disappointment with a specific scheme or ability. Avoid including others who were not involved in the failure. Sometimes coaches will give negative feedback to the entire team when it is really a specific group that has underperformed. This results in uncertainty and mixed messages to the team. We lose credibility as leaders when this happens because the team questions our ability to evaluate situations. When we are specific, there is no guessing and team morale is better. The challenge is to deliver messages on how to improve without being divisive.

D)   **Be prudent** – "Praise in public, chastise in private". This statement goes a long way in sport. When we praise our people publicly it goes a long way to developing confidence. It is an excellent motivation tool. Most people want to be recognized publicly for their efforts. It may be something as simple as saying "good job" in front of other teammates. As leaders, this is a fairly easy thing to do. We must work at developing ways to do this in a more structured way. It is much easier to do this in professional sports because there is always a camera in front of you.

"Chastise in private" is a much tougher task. How many times have we seen a coach or player berating a teammate in a public forum? This may be the most demoralizing thing that can happen to any individual. Not every player is capable of handling this type of feedback. I have often seen coaches strain relationships with players and teams in these situations. As I have already stated, we have to say the right things. As much as possible, your approach should be to pull the person aside, or into a private office to make your point. Both singled out players and the entire team will respect you more for doing so and ultimately will be more responsive to your instruction.

E)   **Take it offsite** – There may be times when you give feedback that requires you to do so in a different environment. I have found that when making a significant change in approach or personnel, moving the discussion to an outside venue is sometimes a good idea. Being out of the office environment can make the person you are dealing with more comfortable, and thus make the situation less confrontational.

I have taken coaches or players out to dinner when it was necessary to communicate a significant change. The gesture alone tells them that this is important, but the respect you demonstrate for them is also important.

F)   **Keep it structured** – When giving feedback, keep it structured. Make sure that the person you are discussing the issue with understands that you want to communicate something very specific. Even when making a quick comment, make sure that your message is clear and understood.

I have seen times when a conversation at the water cooler involved an instruction interjected during the discussion. Later, to the dismay of both parties, it was not executed properly. Afterward, the common response from the coach or player was "I thought we were just talking about the possibilities". The structure of the discussion is critical in allowing people to clearly understand the specific direction given.

Another example might be the interaction between a player and coach in a meeting. When discussing the possibilities of trying a different technique or decision point, be sure that you both leave the room with a definitive and agreed to resolution.

Know thyself
The source of your truth is within you. "Know what you are, accept what you are!"

Once you have identified what your skill sets are and the situation you are dealing with, it will be much easier to navigate the terrain. For example, if you are an excellent teacher and not a great motivational speaker, you may need to put other people in front of the group or use different media types to send your messages. Most coaches use guest speakers to give their team a different voice to hear, especially later in the season after their voice has been heard every day for six months.

It is important to stay in context with who you are. When you act in a different fashion than your personality, people around you will question your motivation. For example, if you are the type of leader that is quiet and relies on empowering those around you to work through difficulties, it is not advisable to change mid-season into a loud micro-managing type of leader. Just be yourself and be consistent. The truth will show as you share your inspirational views.

The inconsistencies in your leadership approach will create uncertainty and mistrust amongst your team members. Furthermore, it will create questions about the confidence you have in your own leadership style. Accept whatever style of leader you are and build on it. The key is to seek to get better every day. Learn to accept the truth you receive in the feedback you are given.

So remember, telling the truth has its challenges. There will be times when you are uncomfortable. It will create confrontation from time to time. The key is how and when to deal with it. Give feedback <u>immediately</u> with the proper structure and direction.

Be honest at all times and be respectful of those around you. That starts with being honest with yourself. Understand who you are, your beliefs, your values, and always try to be consistent in your approach. Enjoy the fruits that come from telling the truth.

∧∧∧∧∧∧∧∧∧∧∧∧∧∧∧∧∧∧∧∧∧∧∧∧∧∧∧∧∧∧∧∧∧∧∧∧∧

The Business Lens *(Bruno)*

What is the truth anyway? We tell the story so many times and we add an extra little thing to it here and there. Then all of a sudden, over time it becomes a lie. Consider the age-old story about your parents talking about their walks to school, in the winter, with no shoes, no coat, no hat, no gloves, uphill, four feet of snow, 100 mile per hour wind, 80 below zero without the wind chill factor, in the dark, etc . . .
After a while, you figure out that it was probably simply a chilly day.

I heard somewhere that we tell about 200 lies a day. Most are what we call "Little White Lies". Nothing too serious. They help us get through the day. It reminds me of the motion picture "Liar Liar" starring Jim Carrey. He would say "exactly" what was on his mind. This got him into a lot of trouble. Basically he had no filter.

Telling the truth is a tough thing because it always seems to take so much time to explain it once it is said. When you own, manage or run a business, you are subject to marketing approaches all day long. Most of the time, the product or service being pitched is of no interest to you.

Being polite sometimes prolongs the agony of ineffective salespeople outlining benefits of their product or service that you can never use or afford. Being abrupt will not be in line with how you want your business to be perceived. Sooner or later you will have to say that you are not interested. Better sooner than later. Do the salesperson a favor and have him or her move on to a potential sale somewhere else.

The major problem with getting to the truth is that time and money is wasted along the way. The art of figuring that out quickly comes in handy in these situations.

In the professional recruiting business, we read resumes and meet people all day long. When reviewing a resume, you quickly learn that some of the content is not totally correct (we call it "Fluff" in our office). It is a form of "white lies". They use terms that excite the reader and this helps their application get to the top of the pile. It is our job to make sure that the description is accurate.

It does happen that people inflate their successes and qualifications when writing and submitting a resume. Here is an example. A candidate who had previously worked with us submitted an updated resume for a new job request from a client company. In it, he now had listed an MBA from a prominent Ivy League school.

We called him to ask why he had omitted this from his previous submission. He explained that he mistakenly "cut and pasted" it from a friend's resume. His intent was to paste only some verbiage and not the MBA part. That was a small error with potentially huge repercussions. It was quickly corrected!

Always consider that someone else in your world knows the truth and can blow the whistle at any time.

Your Past Follows You
I met a group of kids on the first day of kindergarten and we have remained good friends forever. In trying to remain true

to myself, I always pretend that one of those guys is in the room with me when I tell a story about myself. Why? Those guys know me and can tell (or can simply figure out) if the story is true or not.

You build most of your true character when you are young. Sure you can change but you can't change your origins. Playing this mental game helps me to stay true to my origins.

They know what type of musician I was, baseball player I was, reader I was, how hard I tried in math class, what kind of friend I was, how sad I got when my favorite sports team lost in the finals, etc.

It is true that we change, but the past is registered in the great history book and that is a good point of reference. This little mental imagery has helped me on numerous occasions. It would be so easy to tell a few fibs to impress in a business setting. Let's face it, people like successful people. However, the **truth is the truth.**

One of the powerful things I have done with people who work with me is that I show them where I grew up and I try to describe and sometimes get them to meet people I grew up with. Most are quite surprised to learn about my past. It is like time travel. *"I am not now who I was then, but I once was".* We transform to get to our present state.

This exercise helps me stay grounded.

Another great exercise we use in the office is called "My life in four minutes".

In this exercise, we all take turns telling others about our life in primary school, Junior High, High School, Post Secondary and after that. We focus on proud moments and talk about our friends during those periods. This requires no preparation because you know the script since you lived it. Others find out the true meaning of your journey.

Lastly the person talks about why they joined our firm. At this point, there is only about 30 seconds or less left in their timed presentation. It is amazing what naturally happens.

Because they are running out of time, they automatically say exactly why they joined the firm and what they expect without FLUFF. The listeners are always surprised to hear the journey that everyone has taken to get to their present state. They always start asking questions and I encourage them to extend the four minutes in another dialogue at a later time.

In a nutshell, it is necessary for yourself and others to know who you are as you go to battle, and why you are taking on that challenge.

Remarkably, it has helped me grow and surpass goals. I believe this helps because there is no time spent on remembering details of your little lies. You need to remember the truth about yourself. What you've done, your true values, your family, friends, fears and strengths. Without this awareness, it is difficult to build a plan to move forward and to achieve your goals.

Once you are fine with the truth, you can effectively communicate where you want to go and what challenges you are going to face if going at it alone.

Once when we were in Paris, one of the Directors of the company my wife worked with asked me while he was driving us to our hotel: "Are you enjoying Paris?".

He was smoking a stinky cigarette, waving his arms at the drivers, checking his watch, checking his mobile phone . . . . quite the distracted guy I thought.

"It's a very nice place" I replied politely. After all, we had only been there for a few action-packed days of trying to find a place to stay and figure out work details.

He turned to me with a stone cold stare stopping all other actions and looked me straight in the eyes with his cigarette in his mouth and said very sternly: "Bruno" using an extra roll on the "R" in my name to add the drama usually found in a French murder mystery movie.

"In life there are but two things; *"Blah Blah or Fact"*. There is

> *"Blah Blah or Fact"*

always time for both but I now need the fact . . . ."Do you like Paris, yes or no?" he said, always staring at me.
"Yes . . . Very much", I replied sincerely.
"Finally . . . . I get some facts . . . Now let's go for a coffee . . ."
"Do you have coins for the coffee? " he asked returning to his arms waving, horn honking ways.

From that day on I viewed the truth as just that*: **"Blah Blah or fact"**.

In business, "blah blah" is necessary to pass the day and keep people entertained but at some point, preferably sooner than later, the "Fact" needs to come out loud and clear, as popular or unpopular as it may be.

The "Street – Bench – Field" levels of conversation

In my shop, to help in identifying when "blah blah or fact" is appropriate, we have identified three types (or situations) of talk at work—***Street—Bench—Field***.

This is a concept that I started developing for myself when I was coaching sports. I wanted to be accepted by the players but needed to be respected as a coach, as a leader and ultimate decision maker. I found out early in my career as a business owner and coach that being a player's coach, without the proper framework around expectations is not the best thing. Without proper framework, people will sometimes mistake serious discourse for a joke.

Again I refer to "zip" words.

The Street
This is the idle chit-chat that occurs at the work place. It is innocent chatter about the weekend, your evening, sharing a good joke, etc.

This is an important time because this is where you get to know the person for what they are. What kind of parent are

101

they? What type of person are they in the community? How do they spend their time outside of work? Also, it is important to know where they come from. This may seem like innocent conversation but it is necessary to make this time available in order to know true facts about team mates.

This is where a bit more "Blah Blah" happens.
These are low risk interactions that yield significant information about the people involved. Tempo is low and parameters of conversation are wide.

The Bench

To use a football analogy, this is the time when planning occurs. I call it simulation time. This is when expectations are set and we practice what is going to happen when the chips are on the line. In sports, we call it practice or scrimmage. This is when we practice what we are going to expect on the field come game time.

Preparing for this period is crucial. This is why we send invitations to meetings. It is alerting people that we will be working on things that will be important very shortly.
I find it essential for everyone to come prepared for these sessions. Tempo is high and parameters of conversation are narrow.

The Field

Game time! This is where the planning and simulation is tested and executed.

In business this means: Client sales meetings, interviews, presentations and networking. We need to be at our best and always remain professional. This is where the professional truth finally needs to be revealed. You are making a commitment for future deliverables.

No "Blah Blah" or idle comments here . . . just the facts. Tempo is at its highest and parameters of conversation are extremely narrow.

Sometimes, people need to be reminded which phase they are in. We often take meetings and presentations lightly and soon find out that our competition takes advantage of our lack of focus in game time situations.

Looking back on these reflections, I realize one thing. For me, telling the truth starts with being true to myself, of one piece, in line with my beliefs and values. Sometimes, it is difficult to tell the truth for it appears to be a potential barrier to success. In the end, telling the truth has served me well in building a business that is second to none. At DMA Canada, we are recognized as the "Trust-based Relationship Partner in Employee Selection Services". Telling the truth has allowed me to take pride in my life's accomplishment.

Remember to take what you do seriously but remain true to yourself. Take time to laugh, and appreciate the lighter side of life.

Be sure to remember that "there is a time for everything". And when the time calls for it, "Tell the truth. You will enjoy a very rewarding life."

∧∧∧∧∧∧∧∧∧∧∧∧∧∧∧∧∧∧∧∧∧∧∧∧∧∧∧∧∧∧∧∧∧∧∧∧∧∧∧

Concluding Remarks (*Ray*)

This is a hot potato! There are no two ways about it! The sooner you learn to build yourself a solid foundation from where to announce the truth, the better you will be at riding the wave that sometimes arises when telling the truth.

Consider this. If you develop credibility through integrity with your team, they will give you latitude to be the bearer of bad news. If you trust them to have ownership of the task at hand, they will act as adults and be part of the solution.

Each one of us, as a leader, has experience in telling the truth. We have shared ideas on how to consider the various angles from which to roll out the truth. Again, awareness is the key. Keep the goal in mind. Remember that planning for consequences in good times ensures that the truth does not rock the boat as much when it arrives.

In the end, remember the old adage, "short term pain for long term gain". Be truthful with your team, all the time. They will surprise and reward you with unexpected understanding and focused desire to maintain a steady course.

Speak the truth! In the long run, it may be the most important behaviour to support your leadership excellence.

Old habits die hard, and new habits are hard to develop! When considering our suggestion to tell the truth all the time, keep in mind that it is much harder to tell stories than to tell it like it is.

This can particularly come handy as a habit when you are involved in planning. If you make up stories to justify or convince your peers, there will be times when backtracking will make joint (cooperative) planning nearly impossible.

Please read on!

5 - Optimize Results with Joint Planning

(involve those who will execute the work)

> *"Never doubt that a small group of thoughtful, committed citizens can change the world. Indeed, it's the only thing that ever has."*
> **- Margaret Mead**, American cultural anthropologist

(Ray setting the stage)

This element of leadership aims to alert the leader to the fact that much better results can be created if people who are committed to the goal become involved in the planning of any endeavour. Committed here means those who do the work. Indeed, as Margaret Mead points out, change can only happen when people who do the work are allowed to take part in planning how it will be done.

It may seem to be a statement of the obvious, but we encourage you to reflect on your own experience as you read through this chapter. Obviously, we don't suggest for one minute that your planning skills are lacking, just that HOW it is done sometime does not lead to expected results.

It is a well-accepted fact that "If you fail to plan, you plan to fail". Any successful organization or team must operate with plans that enable effective, timely and efficient use of resources. Having well-defined plans avoids duplication of effort or even worst, gaps between various deliverables and deadlines that are on the critical path to product delivery.

One way to ensure that this does not happen is to involve people who are committed to the production of a desired result.

The critical point about planning is that it must reflect a strategy based on available financial and human resources, experience, time, expertise and appropriate skills set. The plans should also contain some risk assessment in order to be ready to shift to a different option should unexpected circumstances arise that threaten to derail the plan or project.

However, these fundamental requirements can be missed when not all the information is taken into consideration during development of the plan. Usually, all information means gathering input from all those who are or will be involved.

Consulting and involving people in the design of a plan requires a definite focus on cooperation and not divisiveness.

Often, people who are assigned to design the plan lack the necessary expertise to lay it out properly, or else they misinterpret the information being provided, or they disregard information provided because this information does not fit their concept of project delivery.

There are also times when people who should be involved are not consulted, engaged or even considered as key in the development of the critical parts of the plan.

Just like a building foundation lacking integrity can crumble, projects that do not include information from people who are critical to the project's success will likely fall short of the expected goal.

We draw your attention to this element of leadership because a leader is often caught between upper management's decision to forge ahead and work plans that are incomplete. The missing information, or the non-involvement of certain people can further increase the gaps and jeopardize the integrity of the plan.

The outcome will most likely be less than acceptable. Usually, the project leader, because of his duty and responsibility to deliver, inevitably will be left holding the bag, having to explain the failure. We have seen many examples in business and in sports.

Too often, the one who has to explain the failings is not the one who caused the plan to be faulty. The plan carried a high probability of failure to meet budget, timeline, or produce quality results from the outset because it was not planned properly or did not involve critical input from the front line.

As a successful leader, you must pay close attention to the information you have, and who has been involved in the planning stages. Joint planning is essential to produce a winning formula. In my career in engineering, I learned a rule of thumb which applies in most situations. To be successful, a project requires chronological or calendar time to be allotted on two main segments: planning and execution. The rule says that fifty-five percent of the time should be assigned to planning, and the rest to execution. Intuitively, that means a lot more time should be taken to plan than often happens.

Now let us look at both the sports and business contexts to illustrate how this can be a serious trap. Ultimately, it can result in significant non-value-added work (recycling, duplication, gaps, wrong information or inadequate assumptions) simply because there was lack of cooperation in the joint planning stage.

∧∧∧∧∧∧∧∧∧∧∧∧∧∧∧∧∧∧∧∧∧∧∧∧∧∧∧∧∧∧∧∧∧∧∧∧∧

The Sports Perspective *(Marcel)*

If you have ever led a project that had an outcome dependent on many levels of management, this chapter will provide some interesting insights for you.

As middle managers, we are often at the mercy of not only those people above us but also those below. The key to success and sometimes survival is to create and maintain influence in the management structure. "Yes, I know", easier said than done.

As a coach or businessman, your greatest triumphs and worst defeats will depend on that concept. Let us take a closer look.

Devise a plan

The concept of *joint planning* (cooperative planning can also be used) refers to all levels of leadership developing a plan for the project at hand. If every level of leadership has input and contributes to the plan, they will have shared ownership of the outcome. This type of responsibility for the outcome should create shared levels of accountability.

Furthermore, this type of effort should encourage everyone involved to support each other and the process.

Take the example of turning around a struggling team or franchise in sports. If all levels of leadership and management cooperatively plan the strategy, they will all feel accountable to the final decision. Each would have different responsibilities in the execution of the plan but everyone would be aligned to a common goal.

The coach would be responsible for the on-field development of the players and strategy. A general manager would be responsible for scouting, identifying players and staff that complement the devised plan.

The president or CEO would be responsible for creating an office support environment, and enabling budgets and communications surrounding the plan. All levels of leadership would contribute a part of the plan to grow this team through various stages of development (similar to a child growing through different levels of development).

The best chance for success comes if all the leaders involved have a shared stake in the success of the outcome. Success can only happen if the strategy is planned jointly.

Be aware of possible pitfalls
Once the plan is devised, a process to achieve it must be established. This process now becomes the key element to determine the probability of success. The ability of the leaders to follow the process determines whether or not their plan will come to maturity (in this case, if the team competes successfully).

Let's look at some possible pitfalls.

If any one of the key leaders ignores the agreed-to process, the result may be less than expected. For example, if the plan for a struggling team or franchise is to develop players through the draft, and the general manager chooses to trade away top draft picks for older players, this may create long term issues as that decision diverges from the accepted development plan.

The coach would have had plans and strategies that involve younger players and may not include more experienced players. The president or CEO may have created marketing strategies and communication plans that send a different message to the fan base. Such conflicting messages may erode fan support.

The foundational plan for the project is now in jeopardy. Adjustments have to be made to align in a different direction; skills and abilities have to be re-aligned; schemes and game strategies are to be modified. The goal has not changed but success can only be assured if the coach can manage to bring these new players together. Obviously, this takes additional time and effort. As we know, delays cause traffic jams. This is one example of how the process can be derailed.

A second situation that is common in projects is how expectations are dealt with. When performance quickly exceeds expectations and the results exceed the planned outcomes by a significant margin, senior leaders may get hasty and anticipate further success sooner than can reasonably be expected.

In the case of a sports team, if the growth is moving along on schedule, expectations stay the same. When periods of accelerated positive results appear, expectations can rise dramatically (just like the stock market). All of a sudden the team is performing ahead of schedule. Now the president or CEO may be projecting higher sales figures earlier, and changing the communications message to the public.

When the team levels off or even retrogrades, there can be times of frustration and resentment. This can create panic and unnecessary changes that can affect the long term growth of the franchise.

For instance, management can decide to make unnecessary changes if the early success is not sustained. This may compromise the plan and reduce the ability of the organization to continue growing the team as a long term winner.

Committing to the process and sticking with it is the key to overcoming diverging patterns of growth. It ensures that knee-jerk reactions will not undermine the final outcome. It will also keep everyone focused on the elements of the plan and allow effective corrections as necessary to help reach the ultimate goal instead of negating the gains already made.

Apply a project management process

The challenge is to ensure proper execution of the plan. There needs to be a structured set of processes (a project management approach) that steers the plan and keeps all levels of leadership on the mark. There needs to be a filter for all major decisions. Each level of leadership should be able to communicate their decisions with each other to be certain they are all aligned on the common goal. This should happen during weekly progress meetings.

These project review meetings consist of all levels of leadership sharing their recent and upcoming achievements and challenges, and reviewing them with the other leaders to determine if they are in line with the previously established plans and strategies.

I have been part of these progress meetings and seen firsthand how effectively the communication and decision making processes can flow. I have also been part of teams where this process has not been consistent and witnessed how it slowed our productivity.

As I have discussed, the key to effective joint planning is creating a structure where all levels of leadership take a share of the ownership for the outcomes. Weekly summary meetings are a tool to keep everyone on the same page.

The question now becomes, what level of maintenance is required? This is mission-critical, because in reality, even if all levels of management are on board, the obligation of accountability often devolves to one person, the one closest to the execution of the plan.

In the football example, you have probably seen coaches, general managers and CEO's dismissed for a lack of results. If you are the person ultimately held responsible for the end result, your stakes are going to be much higher.

The challenges you face as a manager in business, as a coach or executive in football, is that you are never in control over all your resources. So it is incumbent on you to try and pull everyone involved together. One way to accomplish that is to plan jointly so that everyone has clear responsibilities and accountability to the project.

Planning jointly ensures that you maintain momentum throughout the project because you have clearly established ownership by all those who are involved.

Maintenance is a must

Maintaining momentum in joint planning offers many challenges and opportunities. It will always be less of a challenge to find and create time and opportunity to do maintenance work with those whom you lead. They are at the mercy of the schedules you have created. It is more of a challenge when you are trying to connect with those above you in the hierarchy. They usually have more demands on their time from other projects they are overseeing.

It has been my experience that face-to-face time is the best practice. Identify when the best time of day is to have a quick update. Be sure to have a specific point to discuss.

Remember, their time is precious and so is yours. Share your thoughts first, then ask for some feedback to see if your concept is in line with the plan you have collectively devised.

The answer that you get will allow you to evaluate if something is amiss. Be prepared to evaluate the questions and the answers you receive from your bosses. Those questions and answers will enable you to raise your awareness about inconsistencies that may be creeping into the planned execution of the project.

This process goes on all the time in sport. Have you ever watched a football game on television when a team calls a timeout? You will see the quarterback and a group of coaches huddling to discuss a strategy. Part of that discussion is conferring with the head coach regarding the strategy.

Usually, a quick word with the head coach determines if anything in the overall management of the game has changed. If so, an alternative approach may be adopted.

Whether it is an update or a simple verification at critical points in the project, maintenance discussions (progress reviews) can pull everyone involved together and ensure the best execution for the given situation.

These on-the-run reviews are particularly important when the outcome of a project or the standards have changed and have not been properly communicated. The reality of the workplace, in business or in sports, is that not everything is communicated in a timely fashion, yet the person in charge is often expected to deliver a product reflecting those changes.

I am sure that as you read this discussion, you can recall a situation where you were given a mandate to execute a project in a certain way, only to be held responsible for not completing it with changes that were not communicated.

I can recall coaching in an important game where I had specific instructions to implement a strategy to run the clock out at the end of the half. Our opponent took a timeout because of a substitution error. Our head coach made a comment about our opponent's misfortune. That comment led me to believe that his strategy might have changed, so I asked if he wanted the ball pushed down the field in an attempt to score more points. Indeed, his strategy had changed and I called plays accordingly. We ended the half with a field goal and some important momentum.

Had I not enquired if his intent had changed, we may not have been on the same page. Our quick progress review subsequently resulted in a positive outcome.

Regardless of whether you have the information or intent from those you have jointly planned with, you are still going to be held responsible for the outcome of the project if it fails under your watch.

Influence in the management structure
The most complex projects and plans require influence in
the management structure. Some of your greatest triumphs
and most disappointing failures may have resulted from this
seldom recognized aspect of leadership.

When we think about influence in the management structure,
it is so much more than building relationships. Building
strong relationships is always an important facet of any
venture. However, the key to influencing the management
structure is in your ability to set the direction of the project,
then to be able to insulate the process from outside
influences.

It will always be a challenge to set the direction of a project
as a middle manager or onsite worker.

First, the people you are trying to influence usually have
strong personalities and a different agenda from you. If you
go back to the analogy of the football franchise, it would
be hard for a single coach or group of players to have the
autonomy to set the direction. As we discussed earlier,
many levels of leadership are required for a professional
organization to be successful.

So the first thing we should consider before putting ourselves
in a position to lead projects is to establish if we have
similar ideas on developing and building to the people in
management. If not, it may mean saying no to opportunities.

Secondly, spend time backing up your arguments with
reliable data. Provide reasons and statistics supporting your
way of thinking that go beyond your personal credibility.

Frame them to relate to the type of leadership styles that exist in your organizational structure. When outside influences try to infiltrate your leadership structure, re-introduce the data you have supplied and give examples of similar circumstances that have been successful. Stick to your guns. Make sure your information is taken into consideration.

Creating influence in the management structure is the essence of planning jointly. When the best laid plans do not involve everyone with an equal stake in the outcome, success is going to be difficult to achieve. They may have a stake in the outcome, but unless they have authored it, you may not have their support. There will be no room to wiggle when adversity comes.

Furthermore, even if you have applied the input necessary to garner their support, things can change without you ever being aware of it. That is why maintenance is so critical.

Enjoy the process and always be aware of your circumstances. After planning jointly, make sure you review the plan and ensure you are on course to the goal.

^^^

The Business Lens *(Bruno)*

Without effective planning, there can be no expectations of success in a real game situation. In this section, I would like to talk about the elements that are required to produce joint planning, not the technical aspect or the process, but the people or type of persons who will facilitate joint and cooperative planning and make it more successful.

Joint planning encompasses several areas such as: finance, human resources, product development, sales, marketing, facilities development, accounting and legal just to name a few. As a business owner or manager you may be competent in one or a few of these key areas mentioned above, but I have not met anyone who was an expert in all areas.

Bringing in people from different technical fields may seem like an obvious solution. Accountants, lawyers, engineers and such experts understand the technical details of their fields and help us predict the future by encouraging us to follow and implement best practices.

This brings me to the first of two elements that have become important to me when considering how to create a high performing "joint planning" environment.

Balance between Skill and Vision
The key word here is "Balance". It basically means equal amount on each side. Simply put, just because someone is very good at a task does not mean that they can predict future use of the benefits derived from that skill.

A person with an extremely high level of specific skill and an equally high level of vision is almost impossible to find. At the same time, if you only rely on one of the two, you will not reach maximum effectiveness.

I remember working at my father's car repair garage where he employed very good auto technicians. As a matter of fact, my father is the best technician I have ever known. If you needed something repaired, he could do it. I became pretty good too at an early age because he taught me the right way.

Then I started to ask questions like:
"Why don't we build a flying car today?"
"Why don't we build a car that runs on water and converts into a boat?"
The response was typically, "Go sweep the floor".

My questions were not taken seriously. I would then go in the stockroom and draw up plans to build these unbelievable machines. Relatively speaking, I had less technical skills than the more experienced and more efficient technicians but I had more vision of the possibilities.

To this day I maintain that I never became better than these technicians mostly because I was always preoccupied with dreaming of a better way to do things. I could never understand how someone with so much technical talent could not use this gift to create, and not merely repair automobiles.

The same perception developed later in life when I played saxophone in local musical bands. I got pretty good and joined bands that consisted of mostly older and more talented musicians. Thinking back, these players were fabulous musicians. I began to want to write original tunes. I approached several of them and at the time, to my amazement, they were unable to write anything original.

They could all play already created pieces, but lacked creativity. Most of them were not willing to extend their minds to combine unconventional chord patterns, beats, lyrics, tempo, rhythms etc., to create our own sound. At the time, I could not understand this. It was so frustrating that I became more and more disinterested in playing other artists' songs in public.

Again, these musicians were excellent technicians but lacked what I call vision. In this context, I see the word vision as the ability to envision, the ability to create through the use of your imagination and technical skills.

I now realize that although you need very strong technical people to create and move your company, you should consider the differently-skilled and more creative people too. Otherwise, there will be something missing in your joint plan.

Balance between Realistic and Believing
From another perspective, joint planning can also benefit from a good dose of balance between realism and belief. One does not exclude the other, but care must be taken to have the correct measure of both ways of thinking.

Could you imagine if great inventors and creators actually listened to the people around them all the time? It would sound like this:

"A flying machine? . . . Never!"

"Plug this wire into the wall and images appear from this box? . . . . Stop dreaming"

"You are too small to play professional sports . . . . Get a real job!"

These are the same types of responses we get on a daily basis. Many great ideas never take off because we are convinced that it is not realistic. I suggest that when planning a big project, business or event, surround yourself with two types of thinkers in order to optimize your joint plan:

"Realistic Thinkers" and "Believer Thinkers"

Realistic Thinkers
These are people that remind you of past failures and limitations that they view as truths. These people are necessary if you are a person with a wild imagination. You definitely need to be aware of the risks involved and the real possibility of failure. Realistic thinkers are crucial in your decision-making process because they use historical data to help you determine timelines, cost and quality. These are the cornerstones of business. However, without risk, not only will the reward be reduced but innovation will be suppressed.

Believer thinkers
I subscribe to: "a dream without action is a nightmare". If you have a great idea, stop and write

> **"A dream without action is a nightmare."**

it down, think it through and then decide what to do.

Surround yourself with people who can provide some different skills than those that you possess and you will be able to build a solid plan that will enable you to get ahead. Those same people should commit to the results that you envision.

Word of caution; do not confuse "commit to the results that you envision" with "going along with you". This is why I am careful in not including good friends and family in the planning stages unless they "see what I see" or they have a specific relevant skill.

It's like when you ask your mom when you are young: "Can I be an astronaut when I grow up?" Mom's usual answer would likely be: "You can be whatever you want to be!!!" Unless Mom is an astronaut, she doesn't really know what it takes. This is simply good-hearted encouragement. There is always room for good old-fashioned cheerleading, but it is not to be confused with joint and cooperative planning and creative thinking.

Courage Versus Desperation
Make sure that you can identify the difference between courage and desperation when considering members of your planning team.

In the professional recruiting world, when the economy is down, people can come across as courageous. In reality, they are desperate to get a job . . . . any job. They have learned to say what they have to say to get the job. Courage enables them to stay the course when it comes to their vision of their careers.

Some of the best people that I have interviewed had the courage to state that they will do this job for a period of time and then will move on. This amount of clarity sometimes frightens potential employers because the candidate is saying he may soon leave.

I have been able to justify considering such people by aiming to surround myself with the best available people, and asking the question, "If I had a hockey team and Wayne Gretzky in his prime was available and willing to play with our team for "only" one season, should I hire him?" You can play out the rest and debate it for a bit. Ideally, you would include only the most courageous professionals in your planning group.

In the end, make sure that those in your joint planning group have your back and that they are loyal to you, the team and the goal. It pays to align the team first then take the required action to meet the goals.

∧∧∧∧∧∧∧∧∧∧∧∧∧∧∧∧∧∧∧∧∧∧∧∧∧∧∧∧∧∧∧∧∧∧∧∧

Concluding Remarks (*Ray*)

There is overwhelming evidence in all walks of life that cooperation beats competition within a team, and that planning ensures the greatest potential for success.

In 1992, Charles Garfield dedicated a whole book to the analysis of cooperation versus competition. *Second to None: How Our Smartest Companies Put People First*[25] describes the success and sustainability of those organizations that put top value on their people. The concept is now even more applicable as we find out that technology is not the whole answer to increased productivity.

---

[25] Garfield, Charles A. *Second to None: How Our Smartest Companies Put People First*. Business One Irwin. Homewood, Illinois 1992

Whether we get caught up in daily activities or we lose focus of the ultimate goal and get distracted from the planned pathway, failing to plan jointly (involving people) most likely results in a shaky foundation for activities related to a project. The outcome usually produces results that are less than expected.

There is no reason to allow ourselves to be caught in this trap! It only takes joint and cooperative planning and a will to follow the plan. Usually, that leads to the best results. Of course, it will mean changing some preconceived ideas and opening your mind to the concept of expanding the pie. Instead of dicing and cutting for everyone to have a meager share, think win-win. View joint planning as the opportunity to really benefit from everyone's input. Oh yes, it will take more time. But the time saved in the end, will more than make up for it. Reduced duplication, gaps and recycles will mean more efficient execution, and likely, more satisfaction for everyone involved.

When everyone is involved, collective intelligence is at its best, and the synergy thus created aligns everyone to the common goal. Following the process becomes a guarantee of success. Take time to think about this one!

It is a critical element to ensure that your efforts are well-supported and integrated into the overall plan. If you have joint planning, no matter the obstacles along the way, you will be successful in reaching the desired goal. And you will ensure minimal effort for maximum results.

However, your joint planning effort will have a greater impact if you pay attention to the next discussion – clarity of vision leads to success.

A clear and common understanding of what success should look like will increase the effectiveness of your plans.

6 - Clarity of Vision Leads to Success

(If you know where you're going, you'll get there.)

> "Success is not for the timid. It is for those who seek guidance, make decisions, and take decisive action."
> — **Jose Silva,** American parapsychologist and author

(Ray setting the stage)

In this discussion, we underline the fact that many people fall in the trap of aiming for success but never really defining what success means for them. Success can simply be achieving what you set out to do. For example, winning a championship in sports or closing a big deal in business and making it a profitable venture.

But that does not really pinpoint what would describe the desired result accurately. As Joe Silva said, success goes to those who " . . . take decisive action." But decisive action can only happen if we have clarity of vision about the end product.

Perhaps, a quote from Henry David Thoreau[26] may help to capture the essence of the concept that leads to a clear vision. Thoreau said: "The secret of achievement is to hold a picture of a successful outcome in the mind." Before any success can happen, the image of what it will look like has to be imagined and maintained. In peak performance, everything starts and ends with a clear vision of the outcome. Ask any top level athlete; they will answer, "Success is all in the ability to preview the mental image of the performance".

Many leaders live to regret omission of a clear vision when they arrive at the end of a project or a season in sports. They realize that they could have had much better results with the resources they had to work or play with if everyone was guided by a detailed image of the desired success. They just forgot to clearly define the vision of the end result. Just aiming for a championship will not provide the detailed activities required to achieve such a result.

Consequently, it was difficult to share the total vision with the team, let alone keeping the picture in mind and remaining aware of the steps that would shape the road to that goal. They omitted the singular recognition for contribution, or failed to use all the potential at hand because in the moment, it seemed that what a team member offered (idea or other useful suggestion) or activity that was accomplished was not totally connected to the end goal. Hence it was disregarded,

---

[26] Thoreau, Henry David. American author, poet, philosopher. 1817-1862.

or worst yet, the originator was reprimanded for not being focused on the job.

Another aspect to consider in this discussion is the failure to share the information for the necessary steps with the team members. The leader expects them to pay attention and execute the steps properly. As people of good will try to do their best, they act without key information and come up short on delivering what the leader expected.

And yet, the lack of performance was due in large part to the leader's inability to establish clearly what milestones would be reviewed, thereby reducing the people's ability to take responsibility and be accountable in a timely fashion.

How often do expectations reside only in the leader's mind? And when they are called for accounting, the leader hopes that the team will have done what was expected. At times, the results will fall short and negative feedback follows. To the naked eye, the modus operandi of the leader seems to be "Read my mind, and if you miss, be ready to suffer the consequences!"

To avoid such problems, here is a suggestion that can eliminate a number of these disconnects along the way. Take a project management approach and lay out a Gantt Chart[27] for your project; share it, explain it, and make sure everyone

---

[27] The chart is named after Henry Gantt (1861–1919), who designed it around the years 1910–1915, to support war preparations. A software produced by Microsoft called Microsoft Project can be very useful in laying out a project plan. Although it has limitations, it is a tremendously helpful tool to communicate what has to be done in a timely fashion by whom – a clear picture of success. It also provides measurement of the progressive achievement of the goal. More can be learned about Gantt Charts using a Google Search.

understands his or her role. Define what success will look like with clearly marked interim goals/milestones at critical points. Share the vision of a successful completion.

Using a Gantt Chart helps to keep focused on every step of the way of a project or plan, and is a sure way to regularly measure progress. Over time, it enables the whole team to contribute and achieve the vision of success that was designed at the start.

A clear view of the end product provides a constant focus that helps reduce waste along the way. Success then becomes a self-fulfilling prophecy.

Now let us look at how sports and business design their vision of the future, and work to ensure success.

^^

The Sports Perspective (*Marcel*)

How we design our vision of success is ultimately what provides us with the feeling of satisfaction in every area of our lives. Everyone gets excited when they accomplish a goal or feel they have succeeded at a task. As human beings, we have to fulfill that craving throughout our lives to be truly happy.

In football or any other sport, we are defined by wins or losses each week. We are always chasing championships to determine our place in history. Anything short of that, and we tend to see ourselves as unsuccessful. However, even in failure, there is opportunity to grow. I will share more on that later.

As a coach, I have been part of championships and other memorable wins. I have also been part of losing seasons and disappointing losses. At season's end, I always do an evaluation of the year. The irony is that some of my better coaching jobs have come from seasons where the results were not considered successful from the standpoint of winning at the highest level.

So I have to ask the question, was this a successful year? What determines success? What are the measuring sticks? Is my personal success always tied to the results of the particular team or organization that employs me?

Have a Goal

One of my favourite definitions of success comes from Earl Nightingale. He states "Success is the progressive realization of a worthy goal." This basically suggests that any person engaged in a valuable activity is successful.

This has great meaning to me because it provides the insight needed to recognize that no effort is in vain if it aligns with the end goal.

If you first look at success from a personal level, there is obviously an end goal and achievement that you wish to accomplish. However, as my coach (Ray) often reminds me "the goal is not at the end of the road, the goal is the road."

To reach the end goal, there are a number of milestones and interim wins that allow measurement of progress. In some cases, that ability to measure can provide more satisfaction than the attainment of the final goal.

As a coach, my career as a leader belongs to me and the job I am in belongs to my current employer. The first step to being successful is having a personal clearly-defined long term goal. This goal has to be worthy and aligned with your skills, desires and resolve. Once this is established, anytime you are taking steps to work towards that goal, you will be successful. After all, only one team wins the championship each season after many interim wins have been reached along the way. And there are only a certain number of promotions each year in your field.

However, if your personal success each year is based on the final outcomes, you may fail more often. Personal success must be assessed with a different set of criteria.

Personal Growth Determines Success
In my view, personal growth is the number one determining factor for evaluating my level of success each year.

On the whole, I would consider personal growth as learning new skill sets, dealing with new challenging situations and being exposed to different environments. Any year that I could acquire further knowledge from any of these areas was one considered to be successful. These learning opportunities come from filling our role and the natural progression of our time in any position.

During my first years as a head coach at the collegiate and professional levels, just focusing on the new administrative responsibilities created growth opportunities. That learning began well before I ever coached a football game. Promotions and transitions are often accompanied by growth through responsibility.

The challenge is "When and how do you create the opportunities to grow?" Demonstrating success and readiness for promotion comes from periods of personal growth.

Once, I voluntarily left a coaching position for a lower level position with another organization. It was a time in my career when I needed to learn and grow if I was going to continue to successfully chase my goals and dreams of becoming a head coach.

That year, I learned from other coaches and administrators who provided me with additional knowledge and insights to be promoted beyond my previous coaching level. The change provided me with the opportunity to learn new skills and systems, deal with new challenging situations, and I was exposed to a different coaching environment.

This was a unique opportunity to grow in all three areas. I had to have the faith that the move would be best for my career development. It is always challenging to move from the present to the future because tomorrow is not a certainty. It takes a firm commitment to the goal and a readiness to focus on the interim goals. Remember the goal is the road.

Before my last year at the collegiate football level, I spent an inordinate amount of time engaged in professional development. I visited National Football League training camps, watched videos, read books on leadership, and spent time with my performance coach designing a strategy to enable the best use of my skills as a Head Coach. Going into training camp that year, I was concerned that I did not spend enough time on campus taking care of the many little things that are necessary to win a championship.

As the season went along, I had to deal with a number of team and individual situations, and the challenge was greatly reduced by my study and preparation during the off-season. We ended up winning a national championship.

I am convinced now that the time I spent growing as a person had a greater impact on our team than I would have thought. I realized how much expanding and solidifying my abilities to listen, communicate my expectations effectively, delegate tasks to my assistants, organize our team process, share my vision, provide feedback in a specific and timely way, take corrective action when required, and celebrating successes along the way helped me as a leader to create a championship environment.

Conversely, I also experienced years where working tirelessly as a coach and putting all my focus on developing schemes and plays, creating football strategy and situational analysis, and searching for key players that would execute that plan led to minimal growth. My football skills grew but my personal development was barely incremental. On the whole, this did not serve me or my organization as well as a more balanced approach to leadership.

When you create a vision that defines how you will personally be successful, your eyes will always be on the goal. A better you, is also a better asset for your current organization.

Establish Measurement Criteria

When leaders are defining success in their current positions and organizations, they must have some measurement criteria.

If those criteria were to win the championship in a season or finish first in sales, it would be tough to go through every football season or yearly evaluation seeing that your efforts were regarded as a failure.

I am not talking about seeing the glass half full or accepting mediocrity. We must be aware of certain realities when we evaluate an outcome. Did we have the necessary tools? Were the environment, organizational structure and work conditions present to be successful in that place? Was there an unexpected and significant market shift at play?

Many factors can affect organizational output and ultimately how our efforts to be successful are viewed. Often, those factors are out of our control. But there are two fundamental measurement criteria that I have considered to be of great importance in my career. First, was the organization in better shape when I left than when I arrived? Secondly, did I provide a positive investment in the careers and lives of those I worked with? To me, these are the quintessential measures of lasting leadership.

Leaving an organization in better shape than when you inherited it is allows one to use traditional empirical evidence to measure success.

As a head coach, I have had the opportunity to take over a team that had some success in previous years but had not been able to win a championship. Through the application of leadership skills and effective action to empower the coaching staff and players on the team, I enjoyed the reward of that elusive championship as their leader. That victory confirmed that I was leaving the team in a better position than when I inherited it.

This is the same as taking over a successful product line and succeeding in pushing it to number one in the market.

I have also had the opportunity to take over a team that was consistently bad. When I left, we had not yet won a championship. However, the record had improved significantly. The team made the playoffs each season. The team had post-season success. The data supported my criteria of leaving the organization in a better position than when I arrived.

Again, this example can be related to taking over a sales division of a company that is performing poorly. The company may not achieve the number one ranking during your tenure, but if market share and sales percentages improve, these measurements reflect company success.

Help Others to Help Yourself
Investing in the careers of others has always been an excellent indicator for me to evaluate whether I have been successful during my tenure in an organization. There is a bible verse that, when translated, states "A good tree bears good fruit".

138

What do you contribute as a leader? Are you developing quality individuals, employees, leaders? As a coach, I am always excited to see our players and coaches being promoted, whether it was college players moving on to the professional level or CFL players moving on to the NFL.

I make it my mission to help them reach their personal goals even at the expense of losing good quality people. Nothing motivates people more than knowing their managers are taking an interest in helping them move beyond their current level of responsibility or financial compensation.

I have also had the privilege of having assistant coaches promoted to head coaches. These departures usually take time and effort to replace. The positive aspect is that when your personnel are being promoted internally or externally, ambitious people are attracted to your organization.

Usually, people get promoted based on their abilities and performance. Your contributions as their leader may vary in each situation. It may be the work environment which you establish. It may be investing time to help employees improve their technical skills. Sometimes it is as simple as being a good cheerleader, giving positive feedback freely. However, for the most part, your contribution is a combination of many actions that support and enable people to be all they can be.

If you bear good fruit, you will always be successful. Making efforts to help others grow and develop their potential is a sure way to help your own cause. If your people grow and move up, you will certainly have an easier time of growing in your career.

Have a Greater Purpose
A chapter that talks about clarity of vision leading to success would not be complete without some discussion around taking a holistic approach to our professional lives.

There are two areas which relate to my personal and professional success wherever I have been. The first is simply being able to say that I worked with integrity. The second is being able to say that I had a positive impact on the community. In my estimation, when you leave any project and can confidently make both statements, then you have been successful.

Integrity
Integrity has different meanings for different people. I often tell our players "integrity is what you do when no one is looking". As leaders, this becomes a much more complex question. So here are some of the questions/criteria I have found to be important in establishing my integrity in a specific situation:
- Did I put forth the time commitment this project required?
- Was I enthusiastic and energized each day?
- Did I put the organization's needs ahead of my personal goals?
- Did I support everyone involved in the project?
- Did I set the proper example?
- Was I consistent?

These questions could be the subject of another book.

Right now, let us review each and reflect on how they affected my behaviours.

If you can be honest with yourself and walk away from any project being able to confidently say that you put in an honest effort with enthusiasm and respect for everyone on a consistent basis, you worked with integrity. If you analyze some of these questions, they have some real challenges.

For example, when you put the organization's needs ahead of your personal goals, it will not always be in your best interest.

Professional sports are a domain that is results-oriented. Winning is the only thing that keeps you in good standing. Having integrity will serve you well, but it does not always keep you in good standing. I have seen good coaches and managers develop teams and build organizations. They are hired and fired based on performance measurements set by others.

In performance-based industries you are only as good as the previous quarter.

That is why many coaches and managers tend to make decisions that will increase the chance of having a better record earlier in their tenure. This also relates to business, whether it is a financial services company building a portfolio for an investor or an advertiser building a product profile, there will be pressure to produce results earlier regardless of how it gets done.

Are you willing to do what is right, regardless of how it may affect your standing? It is not always easy to put an organization's needs ahead of your personal goals.

Supporting everyone in a project is also a challenge at times.

This is especially true when you are aware that not all your colleagues are working with integrity. The truth is that many people work with different agendas. Some are out to acquire power. Others are trying to make as much money as possible. Then there is always a group that is strictly just trying to maintain their own position in the organization.

When you are walking past the water cooler, and there is a group complaining about the boss or some employee, are you going to confront them, walk away or join in? This will determine if you work with integrity. If you are invited into a private meeting, will you support those around you? What if you are not being supported, will you derail the efforts of the group rather than trying to find a workable solution?

When we overcome these types of challenges, we truly work with integrity. We fight off the illness that can undermine the efforts of the most willing team members.

As a coach, when you see good teams perform below their abilities, these types of activities are probably occurring somewhere in the organization. It may be at the player, coach or management level. If you ever find yourself in such an organization, work with integrity. Be a leader with a clear vision. Strive to be a positive influence that helps the organization minimize the impact of some dysfunctional team members.

Community Involvement

Improving the community or environment you work in is an excellent indicator for defining success along the way.

Providing positive influence in our communities and workplaces will ultimately leave a legacy. Each different position you hold will give you a platform to create some positive influence. Participating in the community is important, whether it is just treating others well or getting involved in a worthy cause.

For example, I have always tried to do what I could to support the Athletes in Action ministry in the city in which I was employed. They provide an excellent service for players and other interest groups in professional sports. My way to support their effort was to plan times in our schedule to allow players and others to participate in the ministry meetings. I also guided those players who expressed their desire to get involved to join the local organization and be mentors for youth in the community.

How many excellent stories have you heard about professional athletes giving back to their communities? I hope the answer is many. As much as professional athletes are focused on their sport, and are not always viewed in the best of light, most somehow share their time with the community when they are given guidance by their organization. These are the type of activities that make a difference beyond the workplace.

Impacting the community we work in is to our benefit. At some point in time, a family member or a friend may be in need of assistance. The community concern and care will be welcome. We must do these activities with no expectations. It is a matter of doing the right thing.

I have shared my perspective on clarity of vision. I believe it is simple but tremendously helpful in building a successful life. I hope you find the same on your path to leadership excellence.

∧∧∧∧∧∧∧∧∧∧∧∧∧∧∧∧∧∧∧∧∧∧∧∧∧∧∧∧∧∧∧∧∧∧∧∧∧

The Business Lens *(Bruno)*

For a moment, pretend that you have gone on a trip to Disneyland. Imagine that upon your return, your friend asks you the following question:

"How was your trip?"
You answer: "Pretty good".
"Why was it just pretty good" your friend continues.
Your answer could be something like this:
"It was too cold"; "It was too expensive"; "It was too crowded"; "Too many kids."

Then you friend continues: "What did you expect when you left?" To which you reply: "Pretty much what it was".

What your friend should then say is: "Sounds like a successful trip to me. You got more than you expected!"

When designing a vision to establish what success will look like with your team or organization, ensure that you know what the defining activity means. First of all, consider that it is to *discover and set forth the meaning of your project or initiative.*

Secondly, *to determine or set down the boundaries of* the behaviours: key performance indicators, production matrix, communication protocol, milestones and of course how to celebrate once it is achieved are all necessary to ensure that everyone involved becomes engaged, and at the end, enjoys the satisfaction of a job well-done.

Discover and set forth the meaning of your project or initiative.

In our team, we spend time at this point dialoguing about what we want to achieve: What does it look like? How it will benefit? Why will people want to use it? How much will it cost? How much will we profit?

"Discover" is the part of the dialogue that may have the look and feel of a brainstorming session. Ideas flow quickly when this method is used. Possibilities are discussed and the dialogue is high. Creating a common goal occurs during this time.

In a session I had with a company, they did not speak of money or profit or costs. Instead their goal was to be EXCELLENT. This made me feel good inside because when I deal with kids in amateur sports, I encourage them to focus on things that will make them excellent and not to focus on the score or rules of the game.

I have always maintained that if you would put words like beginning, practicing, winning, losing, good, bad and excellent on a continuous line, excellent would be at the end of that continuum. Therefore, all the other things mentioned are a function of becoming or being excellent.

I say that *"**Winning happens on the way to being Excellent**"* and *"**Winning gets in the way of Excellence**"*.

This particular company spoke of ways to become excellent at sales, marketing, customer service and production. Interestingly enough, they also said that they wanted to help others on the team to become excellent in their areas of expertise.

They did not speak of financial performance or production numbers. Rather they discussed and planned how to effectively communicate, train, coach, learn, share and collaborate in an excellent way.

I normally do not attend the actual financial and production meetings but this time, their leader asked me to attend only to observe the communication behavior.

I was very impressed by the fact that they used the exact method we used the day before. The leader was not focusing solely on what numbers they were planning to achieve but also on how the behaviours of the team members would directly impact these numbers. Interestingly enough, by the end of the session, they planned to reach higher level results than the manager had originally targeted.

When I re-visited the group over a year later, they had surpassed this level by over 20 percent. They maintained that it was not what they did but HOW they did it that provided the most satisfaction.

"Meaning" is when personal and business values are discussed, challenged and put to the test. Why is it worthwhile to spend time and money on this effort? Will we be able to truly endorse and live with our results? The answers you produce as a team should enable you to take a direction that inevitably brings the desired results.

Set down the boundaries

Once we know where we are going and why, we would then look at how to get there and what we do once we get there.

This is when we discuss and agree on how we communicate within the group and decide how to deal with the situations when we do not meet organizational expectations. It is the boundaries that we set that keep our team between the guardrails of the proposed ethical and performance roadmap.

It is essential that discussions occur on a regular basis with appropriate messages. To communicate with externally and internally vested groups, the content will be different. Make sure to take this into consideration.

In my workshops, I call this "Press conferencing". This occurs after we have determined what we want to accomplish and why. Then we establish and practice our responses to questions or comments that we may get from people who were not part of this event. The first response we discuss and work on is what to say when we immediately leave the room and see someone from our organization who did not participate in the goal-setting session.

The example I start with is: imagine leaving this room and someone says "where have you been the past few days?" What do you say?

It is quite interesting to hear the unrehearsed responses in the controlled environment of "Press conferencing". They vary from: "None of your business" to "Not much really". Each of these can have negative lasting effects on our team and initiative if they are not crafted in a positive way.

The team spends time discussing and building acceptable and timely responses to deliver to the people outside the group. The next morning, we meet as a group and discuss what comments we received the previous evening and how we responded. It usually is a revealing exercise.

This is also true in the sports world when the reporters are waiting for the athletes outside the dressing room looking for a sound bite. We use a form of role-playing.

Some find this difficult and basic at times, but it works. We call it "SIMULATION". In other words, practice, practice, practice and never take chances with spontaneous remarks.

You are representing the team and not just yourself. Therefore, in crafting your vision to define what your success will look like, make sure that you are able to not only verbalize the actions and behaviours that will be necessary but also be ready to act that way every day on the road to your end goals.

^^

Concluding Remarks *(Ray)*

After reflecting on your past successes, don't you find it amazing that regardless of the perspective, you always end up in the same place when measuring success? Has it become obvious that you must start with a clear vision of the desired future?

There are some fundamental pre-requisites if the measurement will be meaningful. Fundamentally, the human factor plays a big role in being successful. Try as you may to make it a mechanical venture, measuring success really comes down to the accomplishment of a worthy goal.

And "worthy" can only be measured against beliefs and values. The bottom line is that, no matter the task or project, it is always completed by human beings with aspirations, ambitions and feelings. And human beings respond better when there is a clearly defined and shared vision of what success will look like.

In order to get the best from everyone involved, you have read about experiences from Marcel and Bruno that remind us that the key to success is to be very clear on what we seek to achieve. Only then can we as leaders enroll our team and help them buy into the value of the end product.

Consequently, a successful leader will keep his team focused on the process, the journey, the pathway that day after day moves them toward the realization of that worthy goal, the pre-determined vision.

As Frosty Westering[28] said, "The goal is not at the end of the road, the goal is the road". And paying attention to the road ensures success in the end, the achievement of the vision. Taking time to establish measurement indicators for each critical step along the way ensures that the process (following the road) is correctly and timely applied to produce the best results. It allows a team to march with determination, enthusiasm and confidence toward the pre-set vision.

In addition, designing a clear vision will effectively radiate your leadership throughout the organization or team. Those who aspire to lead will learn from you. By being a model, you will enable them to learn how to develop their ability and capability to become leaders by example, the subject of our next chapter.

---

[28] Westering, Forrest "Frosty". Former football coach at Pacific Lutheran University (1972-2003). One of the winningest coaches in college football (305-96-7). Author of the book *Make the Big Time Where You Are*. Well known for his motivational speaking and his efforts to spread his positive outlook on life.

7 - Leading by Example

(model, radiate, include)

> *"Example is not the main thing in influencing others, it is the only thing."*
> **- Albert Schweitzer,** theologian, philosopher, physician, and medical missionary. Nobel Peace Prize 1952.

(Ray setting the stage)

As Schweitzer states, the best way to impart leadership to the people you lead is by setting the example. It also results from challenging your team to become leaders as you work the daily routine.

Leading by example (generative leadership[29]) is a type of leadership that radiates from the practitioner and is imparted to those around him or her. It is more than modeling. It is forward-looking, based on understanding and clarity of concept, targeting ways and means to enable everyone in the circle of influence to generate abilities and

---

[29] The term "generative leadership" was coined by Marcel during our selection of topics for our leadership discussions. It is meant to convey a clear direction for the type of leadership that propagates and makes a long term difference for an organization.

skills that will translate into strong leadership candidates for the future.

We all have encountered someone that demonstrated this quality. It is amazing to watch. It is a structured approach by which a leader empowers other people in the organization. Demonstrating a will to lead, injecting one's enthusiasm in discussions, using a positive approach, always driving to finish a task, all are visible displays that make a mark on the team.

I can't help thinking here about my early days when I was growing up and learning about farming. My grandfather used to come and stay with us in the summer to help bring in the crops. He did not say much about how to do things. He just got up every morning, had a hearty breakfast, would comment on the blessings of a sunny day, then hop in his overalls and head for the barn.

There was no fooling around. "Make hay while the sun shines" would be his refrain. Oh, he was a hard working man, and he sure took time to show us how to use the tools. However, not a minute was lost harnessing the horses, getting out in the field, loading up the wagon, and bringing that load to the barn. From morning till sundown, he only stopped for a drink of water or to eat his lunch.

I now appreciate the value of his urgency whenever rain was forecasted. We seldom got caught with hay on the field that was ready to be stored. He really taught me how to work effectively through his exemplary (generative) leadership. I am grateful to him for passing on a quality that has served me so well in my lifetime as a leader.

We take time to discuss this quality because there is
no substitute for having integrity of action and values.
Yes, much can be said about leadership and leadership
behaviours, but a person who can act and help others
develop the desire to be a leader is sometimes hard to find.
And sometimes, people in an organization would dearly love
to see their leaders demonstrate the qualities that they are
asked to display, and that their leaders omit to exemplify.

To be a successful leader, a person must not only talk about
leading, but also engage in actions that speak louder than
words. And people respond to actions. The human tendency
is to take a "show me" attitude. People may fake acceptance
of their leader, but in the back rooms there is disregard and
even disrespect for the leader who lacks integrity, and does
not behave in line with the values he promotes.

On the other hand, there are those who seem to have a
natural gift for leading. They may not say much but they
know when to acknowledge good performance. They also
know when to provide appropriate challenges that help the
worker gain experience and grow in confidence.

They recognize contribution and give recognition in public,
while chastising in private. They foster an environment
where people want to be, want to work, and want to make
a difference. And more than anything, they allow people to
be heard; they make an effort to try their wild ideas. They
allow the clumsy tries that result in new successes because
people are not afraid to take risks.

Leading by example is another key action that makes
a difference in the workplace. Sometimes, it just is not

practiced openly because leaders often forget where they came from, and how they also longed for an exemplary leader in the past.

Leadership is required for best performance by the team. It is expected to be present, is desired by the team, but often is lacking. Sometime, the pressure from upper management creates stress that causes bad decisions and behaviours. At times, it is the training that is painfully lacking. People in positions of leadership do not always have the skills and knowledge to do it effectively.

If you are a would-be leader or an existing leader, please take the time to learn about some essential actions as you will find in this book. Become a "leader by example". Take pride in learning to radiate, model and act the behaviour of the leader who cares for the people he has responsibility for, and has the development of their full potential at heart.

Learn to be proactive in applying the skills and processes that create an environment where people want to be, want to work, and want to grow together. Work hard to be an exemplary leader who leaves a mark for those he or she touches. Strive to create your own stories of success in coaching and leading people to a higher level of performance.

Next, let us read what our leaders-in-action have to say about leading by example.

∧∧

The Sports Perspective (*Marcel*)

Leading by example or "generative leadership" as I call it takes on a life of its own through normal daily activities. I break down the process into two key components.

On one hand, this leadership style is passed on through generations of leaders who believe in leaving a leadership legacy. We see this in organizations where generations of family members succeed each other at the helm. In Ottawa where I was born, the McGarry Funeral Homes have had four generations of leaders. The Rome Flooring Company is led by a third generation son. Clothing chains often are led by successive generations of a family. The leader acts in a way to motivate a son or daughter to follow in his footsteps. The same can happen in non-family businesses where that skill is applied with purpose.

The second component is focused on developing leaders from within. Candidates are identified early in their career progression and groomed to progressively take over. This type of leadership and organizational growth is organic and soon takes on a life of its own. No matter who is at the helm, the general direction and values are upheld by succeeding leaders. Everyone works to achieve the goals that have become a tradition in the organization.

What is a Generative Leader?

Personally, I view it as a very simple concept. Generative leaders lead through their basic everyday activities. They simply "walk the talk". However, it is more difficult to do than to say.

The leader must have an established set of values that will not be compromised under any situation. These values will provide the guidance for decision making. They make his/her every action credible and promote consistency and trust from their team. The values and lessons they preach will be easily accepted and adopted by those they lead.

As a coach and leader, I value punctuality. I take pride in being on time for every meeting, practice, bus departure or other activity. One day, I raced out to practice 30 seconds before we were scheduled to begin. The players began playfully joking and teasing that I was near disaster. The point is, not only do the people you lead expect you to "walk the talk", they will also look for you to falter.

With time, our players bought in to the value of being on time. They even began to preach it and walk it. They made it their own. To me, it was a powerful example of how leadership in action can influence the team. I suspect that this value was passed on and down to their families and friends. It was generative leadership at its best.

For leaders who adopt that approach, they provide an example that is more effective than any lesson, book or workshop a person can attend. The ability to lead or carry oneself is mirrored and internalized by those around them. We are drawn to people with inner strength of character who display the discipline to act in line with their values.

One example is the popular pastor from Lakewood Church in Houston, Texas. Joel Osteen often speaks publicly about his fears of taking over his father's church without having sufficient formal pastoral education or training. He did have the experience of watching his father lead the church for many years. He often explains his father's example was key in enabling him to take over, even more so than his preparatory work to lead their ministry. In leading by example, his father provided the values and beliefs that have made Joel one of the leading TV evangelists in the world.

In my sport, there are two brothers who are head coaches in the NFL. The Harbaugh brothers currently lead the Baltimore Ravens and San Francisco 49ers. Their father was a long time collegiate head coach. They are often heard giving much credit to their father for the lessons he taught them as children. When I listen to those interviews, they always speak about what they saw, versus what they were told. As parents, we have an unequalled opportunity to invest in our children's futures through leading by example.

What is Generative Leadership in an Organization?

When one or more generative leaders are part of an organization, their action creates a systematic approach that fluidly works to integrate and align the group, department or team toward the common goals. Their leadership by example empowers the people to achieve beyond expectations.

Generative leadership allows individuals to take initiative, make judicious choices, and apply skills and knowledge in a way that produces the best results. This systematic and organic approach becomes part of the fabric. It is self-correcting and creates its own future. It is remarkable by the effect that the leaders have on their co-workers to create the momentum in a single direction, the goal of excellent achievement in whatever is executed.

This leadership practice also brings about unanticipated outcomes that usually foster further growth individually and organizationally. It lives through the organization and usually will transcend time and changes in leadership if continuity of the process is maintained.

I have been blessed to be part of some good football organizations. The one thing they had in common was that generative leadership (leading by example) was in place or we were working at establishing the concept. Every leader did not assume that his words were sufficient. Instead, everyone knew that actions speak louder than words. We were of a common understanding that our results would be proportional to the will we had to do what we demanded the players to do.

In football, we always talk about winning a championship every season. Then we discuss how to go about doing it. There are a number of values and assets coupled with a well-defined plan necessary to achieve that goal.

When it comes to the execution of the plan, we need the players to deliver the lion's share of the work. So we set standards for them to meet every day (similar to best practices in business).

One area of preparation we pay a lot of attention to is the on-field practice time. We always talk about practicing fast and giving constant maximum effort. It is a consistent method adopted by most coaches across North America. As leaders, we set the directive, but we do not participate in the drills. We instruct our players as far as the required speed (execution) and tempo (transition periods) of practices are concerned.

In the successful organizations where I have been a leader, a number of more senior and skilled players on the team usually have accepted to take the responsibility to show others and work at the desired speed and tempo. They set the example for others by their work ethic and not by what they said. Other players would follow along. Our goal was to create and maintain speed and effort at practice.

That approach illustrated the way generative leadership takes on a life of its own. It was truly impressive. Not only would the practice become faster, it would also become much more competitive. Other players would rise to lead. That competitiveness spawned better communication. The communication created better focus. Better focus resulted in more productive and effective practices.

Leading by example was the key to elevate everyone to a new level of excellence: less work for the coaches, quicker, learning, minimal corrective action, upbeat mood in the team. Everyone wins when leading by example takes root and moves you closer to your desired goals.

How do we become generative leaders?

<u>Disciplined daily actions</u>
Start with the end in mind. Know what your priorities are. Understand what key values are important to you. If you keep it simple and understand where you are going, you will get there with less effort.

10 Discussions for Effective Leadership

Leading by example must be natural and a part of your belief system. If your daily actions are concluded with discipline and specific intent you will be consistent.

I think of a family example. We have a common understanding that there is to be no text messaging at the dinner table. It happens that when we are sitting together for dinner, I have to remind my teenage daughter to put her cell phone away. She has a tendency to forget.

One day, we were at the restaurant for dinner. I had been waiting for an email message. I was checking my blackberry at the table when my eight year old son said "Dad, no cell phones at the table, right?" I said yes, and quickly put it away. I should have known that our family values dictate that we give our full attention to each other when we eat dinner.

This policy has helped my family to stay focused on being together at the table. I can say that it has allowed many fruitful conversations which might not otherwise have occurred. I thanked my son for the leadership lesson. That episode reminded me of the importance of leading by example.

<u>Be unselfish</u>
If you want to be the type of leader that can transcend time, make it part of your value package to be unselfish. This habit may be the single most important thing we can do for personal and organizational growth. When you sincerely put the needs of others first, you will be on your way to being a generative leader.

When others start to follow in your footsteps to be unselfish, your team members will truly support each other. Everyone will want to help others to be successful, and be quick to give credit to other members of the team. Leading by example must take root in your personal life in order to carry over into your professional endeavours.

How do we become generative organizations?

I cannot understate the value of having leaders that lead by example in your organization. If you are short on them, you likely will not reach your full potential. They need to be present at every level. Sometime, you may have to sacrifice on technical skills to get the leadership balance needed to be successful. The ability to lead may have to take precedence over the ability to execute or manage.

I have been in a situation where evaluations were based solely on the ability to execute a job. Leadership skills were not part of the criteria. That left the organization out of balance and unable to work effectively toward its goals. As a member of that team, I bought into that philosophy. While we had some success, we never created a sustainable environment for continued success.

I have vowed to never repeat that mistake. Leadership is crucial, especially when it comes to leading by example.

Generative leaders have skills but their main focus is to share their values. They usually have a solid reputation, a successful record while leading a team or group. When you interview them, their answers will be straightforward and to the point. They are of one mind, to help others be the best they can be by leading through example. They will take the time to find out if your organization believes in leadership by example. They will make sure the opportunity is a good fit for their career aspirations as a generative leader.

Results
When a system of generative leadership has taken root, it becomes self-perpetuating. Leaders usually produce results that go beyond what was originally intended. Their leadership by example leaves a legacy that facilitates the alignment of new recruits and new management personnel. The tradition develops and reinforces itself. It is as if there was an unspoken agreement between those who started the program and those people who come after them. The established method of leadership by example lives on and flourishes long after the originators have left. Changes in leadership have no impact on the process.

There are examples in sport everywhere. The Atlanta Braves organization had multiple years of superior performance since the 1980's. The New York Yankees have a tradition of winning championships. In hockey, the Montreal Canadiens have a long history of Stanley Cup wins. In football, the Pittsburgh Steelers are hated because of their seemingly never ending string of successes no matter who is at the helm. In basketball, the string of successes of the Boston Celtics is legendary. Or how do we view the San Francisco 49ers of the eighties and nineties in the National Football League? How do you think dynasties occur?

The organization starts out with a goal to win a championship or simply to make the playoffs. Through generative leadership, the process takes on a life of its own and a team may win multiple championships. They may lose key members of the organization, but the results continue.

Just look at the five championships the San Francisco 49ers won in the 1980's and 1990's. They had changes at the head coach position. Jim Seifert took over from Bill Walsh. They had quarterback changes. Steve Young took over from Joe Montana. They still won after the changes in leadership were made. Coaches and players learned from watching good generative leaders and the process continued from one seasonal group of players to the next.

This process is similar for major corporations that have stood the test of time. The system reinforces itself with each change in generation and subsequent success.

Challenges to Guard Against

Why don't teams or businesses always stay at the top once they have this element of leadership in place? Some do.

There are a number of examples of companies like Disney Corporation, Procter and Gamble, Hewlett Packard, Sears and Roebuck, and IBM that have maintained a remarkable ability to stay at the top and continually re-inventing themselves. The Boston Celtics and the Pittsburgh Steelers are two sports franchises that have withstood the test of times, and have maintained high standards of success for long periods. However, there are many more examples of organizations that have become dynasties and then fell off that lofty plateau.

There are probably many potential issues that ultimately cause the demise of such high performing organizations.

Economic downturns, changing demographics, new technologies and leadership changes all contribute to create a transformation in the work context that companies or organizations often are not equipped to survive.

In sport, teams fall back for different reasons. Changes in leadership, injuries to key players and draft cycles that produce less talent are all challenges that could affect the continuity of a team.

Keep in Mind
If you are fortunate enough to be a part of a team that fosters generative leadership, here are a couple of areas to watch closely in order to avoid losing focus and weakening your ability to lead by example.

Too many changes too fast
If you are in a growth period with generative leadership, be careful to not make wholesale changes too quickly. If you fail to replace or recruit additional generative leaders, you will be short on these skill sets. Training the next generation of players or employees will be lacking. You will lose momentum in this critical element of leadership. The long term impact may be devastating to your bottom line, in wins in sports, and profits in business.

Conversely, if you wait to acquire new players or employees until there is major attrition or skills have declined, you will be faced with a similar problem. Your succession plans must be up to date. As changes are made, it is always important to identify generative leaders and enable them to apply their skills for the benefit of the organization.

<u>The importance of the big picture</u>
Generative leadership is about knowing and understanding the requirements of the big picture and maintaining the values that help it thrive in any environment.

We can find it challenging sometimes to make decisions that align to the big picture. The daily minutiae can interfere and blur our view of the future, thereby making it difficult to base our decisions on values and beliefs that are the framework for our success. We need to step back and ask the question, "Is this decision aligned with the big picture, or is it to suit the needs of this moment?"

Leaders who lead by example and generate other such leaders always find a way to see their way to the big picture because they have a moral compass that provides the correct direction. Organizations that have demonstrated strong moral convictions will steer their work in the right direction as well.

In the end, any individual or organization that strives to create an environment where leadership is grown by example will produce a legacy. Effective leaders who emphasize leading by example will sprout from within and ensure a common thread of leadership by example all the way from the top to the bottom.

Leading by example will become an organic process that ensures success under most circumstances; the organization will become an enabling one.

∧∧∧∧∧∧∧∧∧∧∧∧∧∧∧∧∧∧∧∧∧∧∧∧∧∧∧∧∧∧∧∧∧∧∧∧∧

The Business Lens *(Bruno)*

Leading by example (generative leadership), to me, means generating a positive energy within your group that will encourage them to keep the momentum going with or without the current leader being present. Similar to an electric generator, it helps create useable energy.

Mental energy is the continuous positive flow of ideas that come from the minds of your team members. Allow them to be part of the decision-making process and they will help you get to where you want to go. Just remember to help them get to where they want to go too.

A good indicator of this concept at work is when we receive calls from people who want to join the firm or who are willing to buy into the firm and work towards becoming a partner. Another indication is when team members start taking more of a leadership role without being asked. They start training groups, networking groups, sales training sessions etc. on their own.

> **"You are in because you want to be in."**

These activities do not just happen. They happen because passion has been promoted in that organization. ***"You are in because you want to be in".***

Identify your true leaders, build them up, and link them with your team members and you will have a high-powered team that is built on true and attainable passion for success.

How Leading by Example Plays Out in Real Life
- How important is the goal you have set for you and your team?
- How much money or time are you willing to invest to get there?
- How hard are you willing to work to get there?

Make sure you know and are clear on the answers to those questions!

Once you know the answers, you better communicate this over and over again so that everyone becomes engaged and aligned to the organization's mission.

Communicate in the form of words, and actions that are in line with your beliefs and values.

Conversely, make sure that you make it clear to the troops if the goal or mission is not that important to you, or it is something you just feel would be nice to achieve but not worth putting any great effort on the line. If you are not truthful, people will figure it out either right away or eventually. They will not be likely to buy in the next time.

It does not matter if you are not one hundred percent committed, but admit your state of mind. Never lie or try to do as if you are. It could backfire on you.

Some of the most effective managers I have encountered will simply state what is important to them. You cannot always be passionate about every project or cause even though you think you should be.

The Essence of Conviction

Accounting has always come easy to me to the point where I thought that because I was good at it, it meant I should become an Accountant. I did not enjoy university life or the courses. I felt like it was an exercise in following a system and not being allowed to be creative. I could not wait until I graduated.

After graduating from University, I enrolled in an Accounting Designation program and continued to do well. I followed the designation path and truly liked it. I can't really explain that, while I really enjoyed the topic, I did not want to be a Professional Accountant (no offense to accountants).

The advanced concepts seemed to make more and more sense to me. I was in my final stage of designation and all that was left was to article with a firm. I would study course outlines before the course began and was extremely prepared for all course contents.

I spoke with a colleague when I made my decision and she could not understand it. I explained that although I understood and appreciated the material, my heart was not into it at all. I learned the concepts so I could use them in another field. She could not understand that.

It wasn't the work required that worried me but I was not passionate about accounting. Now I know I made the right decision for the right reasons. I would have made a poor accounting firm partner and I would have wasted the company's time and mine. I also would have been a miserable person.

This experience helped me immensely in my future initiatives. I have been able to better identify short term and long term partners, employees and sub contractors in order to deliver my services in a productive and efficient manner.

A Source for Leading by Example
You can look at leading by example in a number of ways.

As action words, I would like to share the following concept as a mind teaser in your quest to make this activity real. I hope that it will help trigger your mind when you lose sight of your mission as a leader. To make your organization great, you will want to demonstrate a skill for knowledge transfer. Here is my TIP.

A good company becomes a great company if it can transfer knowledge quickly. When I talk about Knowledge Transfer, I consider the three following areas:

> **T**: Technical
> **I** : Intelligence
> **P**: Passion

Technical
This is the WHAT of "what we are doing or producing"; it is our technical competency. This may be welding, cooking, flying a plane etc. Successful companies document this area extensively for future use by the next generation team members. Time is invested in producing and delivering this material and making it available so that it can be understood and implemented quickly and with minimum effort.

Intelligence

This is the "HOW" to do the technical from the point of view of what makes the organization different in its technical delivery. This may include a step by step proprietary process that makes your delivery unique in the market place.
Again, much effort has been put into the documentation, the clever videos and audio productions, to ensure that there is wide organizational awareness of what makes the organization different from the other competitors.

Passion

This is where it becomes more difficult! This is where and when we try to transfer the "WHY" we need to be <u>IN</u> this business, from an intrinsic point of view. What drives you to be in this industry and in this organization?

This is where past leaders and innovators become so important. We learn so much when we have someone reminding us of the passion that was involved during the building years. Younger professionals may be quick to dismiss the seniors' point of view because they lack the most current technical expertise. Most believe that the game is won with two simple ingredients "Speed and Strength". We forget about "Experience".

Experience is something that cannot be readily measured. Rather, it is felt like electricity going through your body when someone who was there is sharing the trials, tribulations and heroics of the past.

This reminds me of my parents and thousands of others who came to America with a dream and a relentless desire to make a better life for themselves. There was no sense of entitlement but rather a great sense of gratitude to anyone who would give them an opportunity to prove their worth.

No matter how financially successful the next generations become, they do not match up to the passion of these great people.

This is the reminder and the insistence of TRADITION and PASSION!

The Leader's Message
Again, I firmly believe that any message that will incite your team to follow you has to start with your actions demonstrating leadership by example.

The more you remind everyone how much a project or a specific goal means to you and what you are willing to do to get there, the less you will encounter resistance to your vision.

This comes from modeling your best behaviour: always being prepared for meetings, treating others on the team like professionals, listening to ideas and considering them, getting better yourself, playing hard and demanding that your people aim for excellence in what they do.

I have often heard people say that something is the most important thing to them, and the next day, they change their minds leaving those who committed to the cause to wonder where the passion had gone.

In the contracting business, we have worked hard to facilitate contract extensions for consultants who tell us that they are prepared and willing to work for a client and then have them quit to move to another company for a few dollars more.

They usually say "it is nothing personal, just business!" Integrity and loyalty are clearly not part of their personality traits. They have certainly not been touched by the positive side of leadership by example.

The truly great leaders work within an environment of trust and respect, and seek to pass on their best practices by leading by example (being generative leaders).

When someone comes to seek advice or help and you believe that you are getting a true picture of the situation, be sure to share your perspective. Lead by example and freely support and help the person. You never know what level of excellence you may create just by showing the way to good performance.

ΛΛΛΛΛΛΛΛΛΛΛΛΛΛΛΛΛΛΛΛΛΛΛΛΛΛΛΛΛΛΛΛΛΛΛΛΛ

Concluding Remarks *(Ray)*

Once we look at the concept of leading by example and illustrate it with concrete examples, I believe that it **(generative leadership)** becomes a well-understood element of our leadership activities.

It is quite apparent where it takes place. Usually, where a leader leads by example, the level of excellence in results is maintained in good times and bad times. The main reason is that the leadership team is solid, takes its responsibilities to heart, and understands that they are not the only ones who make a difference. They know how to recognize the true difference makers, the employees or team players, the ones that perform **on the field**.

As they go through their leadership routine, a process clearly stands out: they make it a point to identify new leaders, groom them, devolve responsibilities to them, enable them to develop new skills, and more importantly, trust them to be accountable.

They understand that there is no plateau to reach; it is hazardous to rest on your laurels. They understand that the continued and sustained process of promoting the qualities of effective leadership is a sure way to maintain high organizational performance.

Leaders who lead by example generate a leadership-filled environment. They think about the future. They know that leadership can be a changing position. They value succession planning and believe in leaving a legacy through the leaders they have coached. They take pride in watching them achieve and reach lofty goals, knowing that their contribution made a big difference.

More than anything, such leaders are unselfish and relish the opportunity to watch younger leaders flourish under their guidance. They understand that their most precious contribution to their team and their organization is to develop new leaders who will perpetuate best practices.

Leaders by example take time to celebrate the accomplishments of their team and give recognition to those who take up the gauntlet of leadership and show up to do battle.

When you have a thread of leadership dedication that runs from the top to the bottom of the hierarchy, results will very likely meet or exceed expectations. In those cases, you will find that the leaders apply GMP[30] (the Greatest Management Principle), which is "what gets rewarded gets done and repeated". They ensure that leading by example becomes one of the cornerstones of their legacy.

As Albert Schweitzer put it, effective leaders understand that leading by good example is the only way to develop true leaders. There is simply no mystery involved.

Leading by example must be part of the daily routine if it is to exist. That is not always the case, as you probably realize when you reflect on your own situation. That is why, over time, it becomes really important to discuss this element of leadership and make sure it is present in the workplace.

Having reviewed the concept of leading by example, we must mention that there is more here than meets the eye. For one, there is a tendency to assume that someone else, someone like the Human Resources (HR) Department is looking after succession and posterity. Nothing can be further from the truth. Usually, HR focuses on developing the framework, the marching orders (in a pejorative sense) that provide everyone with the reference points for recruitment

---

[30] LeBoeuf, Michael, Ph.D. *Getting Results; The Secret to Motivating Yourself and Others.* Berkley Books. 1989. LeBoeuf has postulated that positive reinforcement is the key to sustained success in execution.

and development. The actual building of new leaders belongs to someone else.

Ah, the big word! DEVELOPING! Indeed, HR's responsibility usually ends at the door of development. It is left to the leadership people to implement. That does not always happen. Often, the daily routine and the focus on the bottom line take over. Little attention is given to making sure that leading by example is in full force.

The other missing link is the measurement system that could ensure at least an acceptable result in that element of leadership. Indeed, when have you seen anything in the performance evaluation you go through every year that smells or feels like a rating on leading by example?

So, how do you ensure that leading by example will be alive and transferred throughout your team?

One of the best ways is to take the time and ask good questions. As Anthony Robbins[31] points out, "the quality of our life is proportional to the quality of our questions". If you need feedback on your leadership, ask questions that will provide the necessary answers. If you want to make sure that leading by example is alive and well, ask questions that will indicate that it is being practiced. Have the courage to listen and accept the feedback from team members. You will be better for it.

---

[31] Robbins, Anthony. Respected Performance Coach and author of many self-improvement programs, renowned worldwide as the guru of motivation.

As you go through the next chapter, keep this principle in mind. Asking good questions provides the foundation for effective action. It is a habit-forming approach that will ensure your effectiveness as a leader.

Please read on.

8 - Asking Good Questions

(creative problem-solving, not hunting for the culprit)

> *"Great ideas, it has been said, come into the world as gently as doves. Perhaps then, if we listen attentively, we shall hear, amid the uproar of empires and nations, a faint flutter of wings, the gentle stirring of life and hope."*
> - **Albert Camus** from a lecture entitled "Create Dangerously".

(Ray setting the stage)

There is a story about Tom Watson Jr[32] that merits mention in the context of good questions. He was well-known for addressing mistakes by people in positions of high responsibility. When one of his managers tried a new approach to a hardware manufacturing process, the test failed and it cost IBM a lot of money.

When the manager was called into Watson's office, he expected a strong tongue lashing and a potential pink slip.

---

[32] Watson, Thomas John Jr. Became the second president of IBM in 1952, succeeding his father and took the company to its world renowned status by forging it into a hub of different units that had singular organizational goals.

The manager reported later that he was shaking in his shoes when, instead of handing him the dreaded piece of paper, Watson asked, "What should I do with you?" The manager gasped for air, as Watson was a tough man. Watson, seeing the painful look, did not wait for an answer.

"Do you think I should fire you?" He quickly followed with his own answer, "That would be stupid. It just cost me thousands of dollars for you to learn how <u>not</u> to do something. I want to regain the cost I paid for you to acquire that knowledge." That was Watson's strategy.

Instead of blaming and complaining, an effective leader takes the opportunity to build on the new awareness gained through a staff's error. Even more important, the effective leader **takes the time to listen to those who are faced with the daily challenges** involved in the service or product delivery. Ideas are incubating continually at this level. As Albert Camus said, most times it is the ability to ask good questions, be quiet, and listen for the answers that brings out the best solutions.

Solving problems requires sustained creativity. Complaining and witch-hunting hardly foster creativity and ultimately, good answers. As Watson taught us, you will do well to call on the people who make the mistakes to help resolve the issues, and not beat them up for their errors or failures.

Often, the leader finds it expedient to call in someone else to correct the problem, or he or she may choose to push everyone aside and try to be a hero[33].

Sometimes, leaders tend to act alone. They forget that other people may also have a stake in the outcome. Under the pressure to perform, and feeling the weight of a team, as opposed to being supported by his or her team, the leader goes on a solo hunt to find answers. He does not ask questions.

Instead, he relies on his network for answers and short-circuits the team's inherent potential. He closes the door on contributions by his people who could share their experience and expertise to provide ready-made solutions, if they were asked.

In this modern age of speed and needing answers "yesterday", a leader is often caught between a rock and a hard place. Upper Management wants answers immediately, but long term results would benefit from some focused and careful thought provided by the people who do the work.

Where do you draw the line? Isn't that one of your challenges? How do you meet both objectives?

---

[33] The connotation comes from the works on leadership developed by Warren Bennis, expert and author of many books on leadership. Bennis stated that good leaders are recognized by their willingness to help people become heroes as opposed to trying to be heroes themselves. The impact has multiple positive effects on the team – enabling initiative, building trust and confidence, strengthening responsibility and accountability, helping to develop new leaders.

If you have established the perception that you are the primary source of knowledge (the hero), and you can deal with issues and problems by yourself, you may end up in an information vacuum. People will not come forward with answers. They will rather hang back and wait to see how you deal with a situation.

The idea to integrate in your problem-solving behaviour is to allow yourself to be **vulnerable**, and not all-knowing (even if you are). As noted in the chapter on empowerment, make sure that you rely on the third cornerstone of empowerment, and be prepared to "ask for help". Be ready to ask questions, and LISTEN for the answers!

If you learn to plan ahead and ask good questions, you will find quality answers. More importantly, you will convey the attitude that others have something of value to contribute. You will reap the benefits of listening and valuing the knowledge and experience of those who are close to the problem. Usually, they can bring really useful ideas to the table.

Please read on as Marcel and Bruno provide their own views on the business of "asking good questions" to find good answers.

^^

The Sports Perspective *(Marcel)*

If asking good questions is a key element of leadership effectiveness, where and when do we start?

Whether in business or sports, issues find us, sometimes at the most unexpected moment. Very often, we will have a tendency to jump to conclusions for lack of time or just by habit! But is that the best way, the most efficient and effective way to get the best out of our resources?

In this chapter, I discuss some of the aspects of a leadership approach that I have found to be extremely helpful throughout my professional and personal life when dealing with challenges. The ability of a leader to ask good questions in a timely fashion is a key to success in this aspect of leadership.

Every challenge presents an opportunity to change some factor that relates to a specific part of your business or professional life. Whether the issue is the result of an external force that you have no control over, or a self-generated problem due to mistakes, improvement is required to move forward. Usually, improvement will require new or additional knowledge or ideas which are more easily discovered by asking good questions.

Let us take a closer look at some of the fundamentals of that strategy.

Know the Reason for the Change
The first thing to do is identify the desired outcome. Determine whether the problem or issue is within one section of the execution plan or whether the complete plan must be overhauled. The desired outcome may be something that changes a specific process. Subsequently, once the change has been made, the new process will help to meet the final objective.

Have a Consistent Plan
Often, we are hard pressed to find the critical answers to move the process forward.

How we find the answers is important. We should use a planned process that is consistent and has some structure to it although some organizations and people believe in the slot machine approach – a random selection – try this, try that, and hope to hit it right.

The analogy is that they try things out just like a person might keep putting money into the machine and pull the lever hoping to come up with the three lemons. They may even change the way they pull the lever, or ask someone different to pull it for them, hoping that the small variations will change the outcome and provide the desired results.

Once in a while, they get it right. They hit the jackpot, but this approach will never provide lasting and consistent results.

Process for Asking Good Questions
If a reason for a change and a plan to execute the change benefit from asking good questions, common sense dictates that we should have a structured approach that facilitates the asking process.

In my experience, the application of the following process has generally produced the desired results in my quest for answers in tough situations. It has enabled me to reduce the time and effort required to succeed.

<u>Organize your thoughts</u> – Find a useful place to organize your thoughts. In football, we would use a large whiteboard. . Coaches would separate it off into the different aspects of the game, something similar to a good call sheet.

<u>Write the desired outcome in the middle of the board</u> – Everything must come back to that. Be certain you have defined this result clearly.

<u>Brainstorm</u> – Write down every idea provided by your staff. Remember, every idea is a good one. How to implement them is not important at this stage. Ask for ideas that are innovative, outside the usual box. Be inclusive; make sure that all members have an opportunity to contribute. Stimulate creative thinking by asking, "What could we do that would revolutionize our sport?"

<u>Identify resources</u> – Write down in a separate area what resources you have, especially those you have not used yet, including those that are not used to full capability. Identify the gaps in resources in a separate area. You may not have everything you need to be successful, but you must work with what you have. One can always ask for the missing ingredients at the appropriate time.

<u>Identify timelines</u> – It is important to know how much time we have to solve a problem whether it is a deadline or simply an issue of execution. In a fast paced domain like sports, results are demanded each week.

<u>Be prepared to change</u> – Before you move forward to solve your problem, be prepared to change. Each person must realize that solutions may require change in the process or

in the members' responsibilities. Remember, "Change or be changed".

Address the problem – If you look up at your board, you may find a complex set of facts and information. The magnitude of the problem will determine the quantity of facts to include in the situation assessment. If you have been diligent throughout the information gathering stage of this process, you should have the information to resolve the issue.

Be adaptable – The solutions that you may come up with will likely challenge some of your staff. Every person must be adaptable and flexible in order to resolve the problem. Furthermore, the solutions may require additional adjustments once you have implemented them. Be prepared to adapt any area of your plan.

Review your plan with management – evaluate the merits of your plan with management. They may be able to offer suggestions to help improve the plan. They may want to contribute to the execution of the plan. This step offers an opportunity to influence the people in the management structure.

Behave with Integrity – There is no solution to any problem that is worth sacrificing your integrity. When asking good questions, stay aligned to your values and make sure that the answers for your story leave you at peace with yourself.

Now that you have a plan to move forward and resolve the problems you are facing, it will be important to determine who will be responsible to execute each part of the solution.

Each phase of problem solving is important. None is effective without the successful completion of the previous phase. It may mean challenging people to take on more responsibilities. It may require people to work outside their comfort zones. Just be sure to communicate all the necessary expectations.

Determine how you will measure the success of your changes. This will start with determining if you have created the desired outcome in the required amount of time. Depending on how much time you have, there should be some interval points to evaluate your progress. The measurements taken along the way will determine whether adjustments may be necessary.

Never Too Early (to identify problems)
It is never too early to start the process of finding answers. It is easier to put out fires when they are still in the trash can. Some leaders employ measurement tools to decide when to consider solving problems. Deviations are immediately noted and addressed in a standard stewardship process. Others do it by intuition, and some just hope for things to improve.

In my case, after back-to-back losses, I always did a complete dissection of the team performance to establish if we were starting a trend. One can always explain away one loss as part of the game. Losses are inevitable in competition. After consecutive losses, our staff would meet to identify any common errors or inconsistencies in our plan, and ask ourselves the good questions that help surface the deviations from the plan, or the inferior performances of some players.

In business, there are quarterly reports that measure output and growth. In professional sports we have weekly reports that show our progress and performance improvement. There may be a greater sense of urgency for us because a season is extremely short when it comes to making changes that can make a difference in the planned outcome. After all, the season is mostly won or lost during the months of preparation prior to the start of the season.

Case in Point
We had lost two straight football games and our staff met to discuss what we needed to do to improve. We evaluated the problems that were identified as the likely source of our unwanted results.

Our main problem appeared to be our inability to score enough points when we competed against the more explosive offensive teams. We put the desired results on the board and began the process that I have outlined.

By asking good questions, we determined that some minor adjustments in play calling were required. That proved to be helpful. But the biggest adjustments came from identifying what player resources we had available to us. There were two players that had very explosive abilities. The challenge was that we had to be creative in order to get them on the playing field. In one case, we had to change the player's position to get him on the field more often. This also provided the space in our lineup for the other player.

The need to adapt a game plan for a player who was competing in his first game in a new position had some challenges, but was possible.

The timelines were tight. We were playing a team that week that had been a top offensive team in our league for some years. The plan had to be devised and communicated before we began our first day of preparation that week.

As the week went on, we created some measures at practice to evaluate the progress of the two players. Some minor adjustments in schemes and strategy had to be made throughout the week, but the execution was on schedule. Management had the opportunity to evaluate the plan and give some feedback prior to execution. Although we had to make some significant changes in personnel, everyone involved understood and embraced the possibilities.

As it happened, we won that next game by scoring fifty-five points, overwhelming the thirty-six that the explosive team we met was able to put on the board. It was one of the highest scoring regular season games. Ironically, that year, we also won the highest scoring playoff game in league history. This was a great team effort that began with asking good questions to bring out the ideas that ultimately made all the difference.

As we have seen, asking questions to find the best answers leads to effective problem-solving. As with other discussions we have seen, too often, organizations and management teams omit the use of a process in finding answers. Most often, the refrain of "we have no time to take the long road to problem-solving" is used to squash efforts to be structured and disciplined. In the end, you have to ask this pertinent question, "If you don't have time to do the right thing, do you have time to do it twice?"

Unfortunately, many organizations undermine excellence by putting too little effort in asking good questions, and in the end, produce results that are below expectations.

The reality is that when a team or organization decides to be systematic and structured in asking questions, everyone benefits. It affords an opportunity to develop the skills to find good solutions to every problem or issue.

ΛΛΛΛΛΛΛΛΛΛΛΛΛΛΛΛΛΛΛΛΛΛΛΛΛΛΛΛΛΛΛΛΛΛΛΛΛΛΛΛ

The Business Lens *(Bruno)*

The discussion here dwells on the fact that sometime, because the leader tends to be a lone ranger, he or she forgets that other people may have a stake in the outcome.

I propose that "asking for help" = courage (not desperation)

In the professional recruiting business, I always tell recruiters that the best answer is another great question. I have fun with this because it seems that it will go on forever. In reality, it takes much less time to get to the answer.

We jokingly call this gaining "In-Fro-mation".

When someone asks what this means, the answer is simple: it is information with an Afro haircut. The more information you get, the bigger your Afro becomes. This is a simple way to remind yourself that you need to grow your information pile just like the hair on your head.

The serious part of this is that the more information you have, the more likely you will be able to make a lower risk decision and receive higher returns. This goes for both the leaders and their staffs. The staff needs to ask better questions to fully understand what is needed. A true leader should ask good questions to clarify his / her thoughts and understand and appreciate the staff's true purpose and commitment.

The more insecure the leader, the less questions are asked.

The fear is that others will discover that the leader is not all knowing. Well, that is true. The leader is not all knowing when it comes to all parts of the planned project.

The best way to ask good questions is to prepare and consider the questioning path as a dialogue. A dialogue includes and encourages more than one person to contribute to the overall idea. It gets easier with practice.

What makes this approach effective is the awareness that everyone wants and needs to succeed in their lives. It may not come across immediately in the project at hand, but it becomes apparent as time passes.

Asking good questions is a natural and instinctive way to gain the knowledge and information to succeed. We all struggle, perhaps unconsciously, to get good answers. I am reminded of this human struggle when I ice skate.

I have been fortunate enough to have lived in the two cities with the nicest and the most unique ice skating surfaces, the

Rideau Canal in Ottawa and the Calgary Olympic Oval. It attracts all kinds of skaters. It is interesting to see the older and novice skaters trying to remain upright and balanced.

They begin to fall and they do everything that they can to remain on their blades. Arms and legs are swinging to return to equilibrium. It looks quite funny even though you know that it will hurt when they hit the ice surface. It would be easier and less painful to simply flop to the ice and then get back up again. Those people fight to succeed in staying upright just like we should strive to find good answers by asking good questions.

Another perspective is the necessity to integrate the concept of helping each other by asking good questions. It is a sure way to extract the essence of what a person needs from staff to achieve expected results.

That concept can be witnessed when you visit the California desert (or any desert for that matter). You notice plants, insects, animals, reptiles, birds, rocks, sand, bones, fossils co-existing, under the impact of heat and yes a little bit of water.

In fact, so little water that you don't see it.
How do all these living things manage to stay alive in an area such as this?

The creatures and plants live in a "symbiotic" way.

Symbiotic (from the dictionary): A close and prolonged association between two or more different organisms of different species that may, but does not necessarily benefit each member. A relationship of mutual benefit or dependence.

In order for the plants to survive, they rely on the birds that will be eaten by the other animals that will feed on the insects that help the trees stay alive and so on.

In the business world, the same principle applies. We need to ask questions in order to create the symbiotic relationship that allows everyone to figure things out and find answers.

This includes competitors, colleagues, contractors etc. Therefore, be brave and ask questions that will get you to your goal. Keep learning. Always train. Always practice. Try new things.

Asking Questions Related to Behaviour
My view is that if you want answers concerning behaviour, ask a five year old.

When it comes to how we behave, we most likely learned all the basic behaviours by the time we were five years old. When you need to act on something at work or within a team, ask yourself how would I want my five year old to behave in this situation? One of the things we coach our kids is that everyone gets angry, happy, tired etc. I It is what we chose to do and say when we are in this state that solves or creates a problem.

In business, if you don't expect to be sad, frightened, angry, happy, furious, tired just to name a few, you are sadly mistaken. We all get these feelings. It is how we mentally practice how to act when we feel this way that defines us as professionals.

Listening to younger and less experienced people is just as important as listening to old veterans. They offer a fresh prospective.

I did say "equally important" as just as many answers can be obtained in the retirement homes of our country. The seniors of our nation built this country and have a world of knowledge that they are dying to share.

Asking Good Questions in a Business Startup
A great way to find answers in a smaller business environment is to create a Board of Intelligence. A few years ago, when I started a new venture, we were too small to have a true board of directors. We just did not have the budget. However, I networked with highly motivated professionals from different fields to whom I asked a lot of good questions. They simply offered their best opinions, suggestions and advice.

The information I received was amazingly helpful. They were brutally honest and forthcoming with their ideas and opinions. That was exactly what I needed. Their knowledge, passion for achievement and desire to help made the startup much more effective and efficient. (Thank you Colleen, Bernadette and Bruno).

The true meaning of asking good questions will be found in your willingness to succeed. The stronger the will to surpass your goal, the more you will stretch in order to seek better ways of doing things. And these incremental bits of knowledge will come readily from your ability and willingness to ask questions.

^^^

Concluding Remarks *(Ray)*

Creativity does not happen by chance. It is a quality that an organization must promote and foster. We must be deliberate and structured in asking good questions to find the answers we need to succeed. Otherwise, failure to do so may give answers which are less than the ones that would make a big difference.

From another angle, I am sure you can feel that there is a great deal of trust required to be good at this.

Providing good answers sometimes requires people to be bold and courageous in bringing forward their opinions, ideas, and unique suggestions. This does not happen freely when trust is lacking. Leaders play a significant role in creating an environment that will allow people to be courageous, bold and ready to share their ideas.

To some extent, we see here how the 10 Discussions for Effective Leadership intersect. If you are going to be good at asking questions to find the answers you require, you have to ask questions that help people believe that their knowledge and contributions are valued, and not the type that make people feel ridiculous. Remember the saying, "the quality of your life is proportional to the quality of your questions".

This implies effective listening, something like letting people answer your questions as opposed to getting impatient, cutting them off, and showing that you are Mr. Know-it-all. It is imperative here to reiterate that effective communications can make or break your leadership activities.

Too many forget and pay dearly for their sin of omission when it comes to listening. By listening effectively, a person will gather the best intelligence, the soundest views and the most creative suggestions to optimize their approach to leadership.

Indeed, listening effectively promotes and fosters collective intelligence. How can one mind be better than the collective mind of the team members? It is a crucial element of leadership built by asking good questions.

Consult with your team. You may be surprised to learn that one of the most desirable leadership behaviours is the ability to listen to and acknowledge what people say. There is no greater mark of respect and trust. It usually provides the key to finding answers.

As Camus said, " . . . listen attentively, and you shall hear . . ."

> *Get the answers you need by listening patiently. Learn to build the habit of turning "impatient" into "I'm patient".*

Finding answers is difficult in many cases, and those leaders who suffer from a lack of support or input from their team should step back and ask themselves, "Am I really listening to the answers people are giving me?" "Am I being patient?"

Asking good questions is an ongoing challenge for a leader. Critical facts and opinions reside within the team members. Work to avoid extracting answers forcefully; it may result in creating barriers to good information from the team. Being patient and listening effectively will go a long way toward reducing potential barriers to maximum performance.

Yes, it takes patience. But isn't it a fact that when you look at the word impatient, the answer lies right within it? "Impatient" can easily be changed to "I'm patient". It is a matter of developing belief through affirmations[34]. In times of stress and urgency to get resolution, tell yourself that you are patient. With time, you will develop the new helpful belief that allows you to listen effectively.

We leave you to ponder these ideas and reflect on the habit of patience as we move to the essence of a winning leadership attitude, the ability to think like a champion.

---

[34] Perras, Raymond. *AïM for Life Mastery*. AuthorHouse. Indianapolis 2011. Available at Amazon.com. Details the technique of affirmations.

9 - Think Like a Champion

(looking for effort-less effectiveness[35])

> *"I have been wounded but not yet slain. I shall lie here and bleed a while. Then I shall rise and fight again. The title of* **champion** *may from time to time fall to others more than ourselves. But the heart, the spirit, and the soul of champions remain in* **us.***"*
>
> **- Vince Lombardi**, famous coach, Green Bay Packers

(Ray setting the stage)

My old football coach Matt Anthony, University of Ottawa Gee-Gees 1968, used to say, "If you wanna play football, you gotta wanna play football." If you want to be a great leader, you "gotta wanna" be a leader. Never truer words spoken apply to a person who seeks to lead.

Vince Lombardi pointed out that it takes perseverance and tenacity to stay the course. But in the end, thinking like a champion is what makes you the best you can be. It is habit forming and with time, ensures that no matter what befalls you as a leader, you know how to bounce back and keep the team on course to success.

---

[35] See page 16 footnote for a clarification of the term.

Here, we are making a statement that dreaming of a championship will remain a dream, unless the leader has a "championship mentality", the ability to think like a champion.

> *Dreaming of a championship will remain a dream unless you think like a champion.*

This is one of the truisms in performance. Many aspire to win a championship, become a massive success in business, show a remarkable accomplishment by the team, any result that ranks as outstanding. The problem is that results are often less than expected because people fail to think like champions.

There are a multitude of elements involved in thinking like a champion. Your personal experience may suggest more but here we want to highlight the following ten:

- Create a vision of the desired future, with sustained commitment to it, shared with your team to inspire them;
- Sacrifice for the cause; be ready to do what you ask the team to do;
- Take no breaks; be relentless;
- Trust your team to get it done;
- Recruit winners; get people with the right attitude;
- Pay attention to details; it's the little things that kill you;
- Give people responsibility and authority so that you may hold them accountable;
- Remember people are people, not machines;

- Demand and expect excellence;
- Celebrate every successful step along the way.

A winning coach, a successful business leader, or any person who is recognized through the strong performance of their team usually has the ability to observe and exploit the value of these ten elements.

It is this dedication that evolves into a championship mentality, a relentless drive to excellence and an undaunted will to show the way. True leaders engage the team in a sustained effort to dream, reach out and achieve the desired goals.

Each element is put into action by a good leader in the following way:

- Personal direction is clearly defined, articulated and shared, sustained and exemplified through actions that instill the belief that nothing less than excellence will be accepted.

- The leader cannot demand that his/her team members do what he or she is not ready to do. A true leader shows the way to a championship. No amount of sacrifice is too big when peak performance is required.

- Thinking like a champion takes mental effort every minute of the day. A championship mentality understands that bad habits can easily be developed. The leader is alert and stays focused on the prize, doing the right thing, and encouraging his people to follow his example.

- Thinking like a champion is demonstrated by the trust and confidence that the leader puts into his team, believing that everyone will perform to the best of their ability. It also involves the leader's confidence that he has enabled the team members to do what it takes to produce the desired results.

- To build a championship team, you have to have the right elements, and that starts with recruitment. That presumes that the leader understands and knows his team and is clear as to what additional players are needed to complete the final make-up.

- Paying attention to details is essential to a championship mentality. The little details receive the required attention to ensure that nothing is left to chance. Indeed, it's the little things that will kill your chances to reach the gold.

- To create a championship mentality, everyone on the team must feel that they can contribute and have a clear responsibility and are accountable for the tasks they have been assigned. If every ounce of performance is to be extracted from all of the resources in place, there must be a method to release that potential. Giving responsibility and expecting accountability will propel individuals to the heights of peak performance.

- The leader who thinks like a champion never forgets that every step to success depends on the good will of the people. Feelings are always in action. Motivation is the fuel and when people are treated like machines, they usually respond negatively. Championships are built on the ability of the leader to empathize with his team, listen to their feelings and build on their drive to excel.

- Denis Waitley[36] suggests that a winning mentality starts with having "positive expectancy". A leader will empower his team by expecting them to perform at the peak of their ability. But he will do more than simply expect. When efforts weaken, he will provide constant reminders to his team to do and be the best they can be.

- Finally, thinking like a champion enables a person to pay attention and recognize success along the way. Every moment of the journey, there is a concentrated effort to recognize achievement. A winning leader knows that "what gets rewarded gets done and repeated".

When a leader keeps these ten elements in mind, the natural outcome is a championship mentality that pervades the talk, the walk, and everything associated with delivering on the leadership responsibilities a person accepted when taking on the role of leader.

---

[36] Waitley, Dr. Denis. *The Psychology of Winning*. Mass Market Paperback. Berkley. California 2002.

10 Discussions for Effective Leadership

The leadership challenge may appear to be a tremendous burden. However, when you step back and assess your role as a leader, the value of thinking like a champion becomes self-evident. You may not always apply the key elements effectively and in a timely fashion. Just know that your level of success is undoubtedly due to the skills you already possess.

When you measure success, you get feedback, and feedback is the key to improvement. Take time to measure. Simplify your life and raise your effectiveness. Work to elevate your team and yourself to new heights of performance by thinking like a champion.

Let us now turn to our co-authors for their perspective on thinking like a champion.

∧∧∧∧∧∧∧∧∧∧∧∧∧∧∧∧∧∧∧∧∧∧∧∧∧∧∧∧∧∧∧∧∧∧∧

The Sports Perspective *(Marcel)*

Thinking like a champion (having a championship mentality) is what sets most successful people and organizations apart from the average. It is the innate ability that allows people to think and commit to do their best each day without reservation.

As thinking like a champion is a habit, it will impact every area of a leader's personal and professional life. Everything the leader does will be seen as a worthwhile venture that demands full attention and effort.

Whether we are talking about a personal or organizational way of thinking, it starts with the people who are in place. That is why it is so important as a team or organization to have leaders that recruit people who think like champions and walk around with a championship attitude.

Personal Attitudes
Thinking like a champion begins with how we see ourselves. It starts with our dreams. Earl Nightingale stated "the size of your life is directly proportional to the size of your dreams". If we work with faith and shoot for the stars, at worst we will hit our heads on the ceiling. This means that if we dream big we increase the likelihood of having a rate of success that will be above excellent. Such dreams allow a person to think like a champion, and entertain a championship mentality.

The next step in the process is giving 100 percent in everything that you do. Our work ethic is what brings us closer to our dreams. People often ask me as a coach, "What do you believe is 100 percent effort?"

I simply tell them that it is giving your undivided attention mentally and physically to whatever task you are working at for the allotted time the task requires. Sounds simple, but it is very difficult to do. Pushing ourselves physically is actually much easier than pushing ourselves mentally.

My dad used to tell me "a job worth doing is a job worth doing well". For example, he would encourage my brother and I to do a good job with the dishes. That concept demands that whatever the task is, we should give it the same attention as our most important responsibilities.

That may mean how you respond to a complaint, how you dress, the cleanliness of your office or simply doing a spell check before sending an email. Aim to create championship habits rather than championship efforts.

I coached a very talented football player for a few years. He came to us with much talent and a great heart. He was a productive player who made an impact in most games. However, I believed that he was not reaching his full potential. His effort and attention level were not always consistent.

He saw other players from our team move on to the NFL or win individual awards, and that made him reflect on his play. He began to see that he had the talent to play at that higher level, or at least be the best at his position. However, it had not happened because he did not demonstrate on film the performance required for NFL scouts to select him for such an opportunity.

During one off season he began to dream about this goal and focused his attention on raising his level of play. His commitment was to start thinking like a champion and come back with the improvement necessary to be a complete player. The transformation was nothing short of amazing.

He worked hard in every practice for the complete season. He treated every area of preparation as the most important thing in his day. He gave his full attention to every film session and meeting. His focus was just as impressive when he was getting treatment.

Most players get treatment and allow their focus to go to other areas. He spent the time visualizing healing, and feeling the treatment. You see, everything he did was done with the same intensity and commitment regardless of the size of the task. His sleep habits, nutrition and mental focus were all equally important. He gave his special teams assignments the exact same attention as his regular responsibilities.

He did not concern himself with office politics. He only focused on the things that he had control over. He became the top player at his position that season, and received a NFL contract offer. That was an excellent example of the impact that thinking like a champion can have on a player.

Championship Organizations

Championship organizations are driven by people who think like champions. They are often present in most departments.

The same can be said about championship teams. These organizations or teams understand that having the people with the right attitude is more important than any other single factor. Once the team is selected, the leaders think like champions and believe that skills at work will bring a championship. They remain focused on what is required. Outside factors or influences are viewed as opportunities to narrow the focus and align the team.

For example, during our national collegiate championship year back in 2000, we were going into a three game stretch against opponents whose talents and previous results were inferior to ours on paper. Although we respected our opponents, we knew that we were going to win these games.

Our concern was staying sharp through this part of the season. I came up with an idea that I thought would motivate our team.

The day before each game, I wrote down my predicted final score and sealed it in an envelope. I told them that I expected their performance to be one of champions. It did not matter who our opponents were. The key was to give their best for the whole game and if they did, the predicted score would hold true. The envelope was given in trust to a member of our staff and revealed after the game.

Amazingly, the players had a deep down inside championship mentality. They focused totally on achieving the desired outcome – playing to the best of their abilities. What was important to them was meeting the very high expectations of performance, and not the score. Consequently, we handily won the three games and in each, we got 100 percent effort.

By the way, in each game, we were no more than five points off the predicted difference with our opponents. It was a self-fulfilling prophecy. Without knowing, the players reached each and every one of the goals through excellence of execution.

Championship organizations have people that give 100 percent individually and collectively. The type of task they are working on is irrelevant. It is the attitude which they bring to the task that counts. They understand that whatever they do has an impact on reaching the team's goals.

As a football coach, we practice three to four times per week for up to six months. That is a significant amount of time. Consider how challenging it can be to have the mental and physical commitment it takes to maintain a championship mentality all that time.

I have been part of teams that would challenge each other to maintain perfect practice assignments for upwards of two to three weeks consecutively. It was not a coincidence that they were highly successful teams. Conversely, I have been around other teams where leaders dismissed bad practices as simply part of the process. Needless to say, these teams were not as successful.

The most successful organizations that I have been blessed to be a part of understood that everything matters. There, the championship mentality showed in every facet of the team activities. Leadership knew that whatever we did had an effect on our on-field product. They valued the efforts of the secretary at the front desk, the payroll accountant, the quarterback on the field. Whether it was travel arrangements or daily meetings, every detail was equally important to our success.

On one occasion when entering the playoffs with a professional team, everyone received a detailed package with an outline of the responsibilities and resources we had available to us if we made the championship game. My first thought was that it was a little premature.

I took the package home and left it for my wife. There were many details regarding travel plans for the families. As my wife has always done, she poured over it and made the appropriate plans for our family. Three weeks later, we were preparing for the championship game and a week of festivities. I returned home after our first day of the championship week; my wife just smiled and said that everything had been arranged. I was completely free to focus on my job.

This was an example of a championship organization that thought like champions. Nothing was left to chance.

If you have ever been part of an organization that has overcome adversity to achieve results at the highest level, you will learn that its leaders have confidence and trust in the people around them. That is the result of selecting leaders and team members who think like champions and are ready to go the extra mile to capture the big prize. Nothing short of that will do.

Their people focus on what they can control. They focus on giving their 100 percent to each activity they are a part of. They believe it before they see it.

Have you ever seen an underdog team win a championship? It usually starts with this ability to think like champions. They do not focus on what they do not have. That only allows for built-in excuses. They believe that they have enough skills and ability to be successful.

However, the reason they are successful is that they practice the championship mentality of being completely committed to everything they are required to do without any influences from the outside world. Our discussion on thinking like a champion raises the fact that, even if it sounds simple, it is probably the most difficult leadership concept to apply. Giving 100 percent of yourself mentally and physically in every task that you do is a challenging endeavour.

Thinking like a champion must indeed become a habit. Otherwise, it will be difficult to choose how to give each responsibility the necessary importance and attention it deserves. Applying the principles of peak performance will most likely help you to reach closer to the full ability of thinking like a champion – **the right stuff, in the right amount, at the right time**.

∧∧∧∧∧∧∧∧∧∧∧∧∧∧∧∧∧∧∧∧∧∧∧∧∧∧∧∧∧∧∧∧∧∧∧∧∧∧∧

The Business Lens *(Bruno)*

A true champion is someone who is doing what others are not willing to do. Once you have set your goal, the plan of action needs to be implemented and performed. This is where the difficulties usually appear and the will falters.

In order to do what others aren't willing to do, you don't need to do things better or faster, just do them smarter, applying the peak performance concept of the right stuff, in the right amount at the right time. The recipe is simple. Think like a champion!

It is all about behaviour and attitude. Ask yourself: "As a champion, how will I behave? What kind of legacy do I want to leave behind? What attitude will I bring to any challenge?"

Doing like others who are average is easy. It takes passion to have

> *Passion cannot be measured. It can only be felt.*

the perseverance and persistence to think like and become a true champion. Passion cannot be measured. It can only be felt. Your task is to develop the passion that characterizes those who stand above everyone else and do the things that make them true champions.

Here is a list of concepts and actions that I believe you should keep in mind to be a true champion:
- There is always room for improvement
- Your strength today—your weakness tomorrow
- Passion cannot be measured
- Practice, practice, practice
- Play hard always
- Know when to take a break
- Listen to other Champions

Let's briefly discuss each concept and action and see how they provide a backdrop for sustaining and maintaining a championship mentality.

There is always room for improvement
Never believe you have built the perfect mousetrap. There is always a better one around the corner. I remind those around me that the goal is not to build the perfect mousetrap, but rather to catch the mouse. Keeping that goal in mind, you will need to constantly improve the mousetrap because the mice get smarter. Remember to not only study the mousetrap but to also study the mouse.

Your strength today—your weakness tomorrow

Be aware that if you label yourself in a certain way, it's very difficult to change the perception you may project. For example, if you say you are a bold person, you are essentially saying to your competition that in order to beat them, you will need to be bolder than they are. I suggest using the word "*can*" and learning to be flexible.

This eliminates the need to *always* be bold. I suggest that you would say I **can** be bold; this gives you the flexibility to choose other options when necessary.

Develop a variety of abilities and skills that you can apply to your effort. In time, that will give you the option to take a different approach to meet your competition. When everything is said and done, only DIFFERENT can ensure that you will win at the game of business. Bigger, better or faster can always be surpassed.

Passion cannot be measured

Passion cannot be measured. It can only be felt. You can feel when someone is passionate about something. It's like nothing else in the world is more important. Be sure that you display your passion in words and actions. Help others feel it. Passion is something that we all have but do not always share.

We are worried about what others will think. This will only delay success. Once you show the passion you have for something, don't be surprised to find out that others share the same passion and will want to join in on your journey to being a champion.

Practice, practice, practice
No matter how good you are, the challenge is how do you get better? Develop a training plan that includes a lot of practice time. No matter the field you are in, if there is no practice time, you are actually getting worse because the competition is practicing and improving.

Learn to enjoy practice time because this is when you can make mistakes and nobody will know about it. Come game time, your improved skills will come naturally.

In our business, those who use role-play for their business calls and meetings beforehand are the ones who are most prepared and therefore likely to be the most successful.

Play hard always
Years ago I played in an All Star baseball game in a men's league. I was pretty proud of making that team. We played an exhibition game against the other division. It was a great event for a local league. Everyone was upbeat and friendly and there were a couple of hundred fans. Not bad for a nothing league!

Nothing was on the line . . . just a fun evening. We each played a few innings and had two at bats. I singled on my first at bat.

My second at bat, I took a couple of pitches knowing that I would not come up again. A fat juicy one came out of the pitcher's hand and I could not resist. Big swing and it gapped between the right fielder and center fielder. I galloped to first and went easily on to second.

Just then the third base coach called to go to third. What? Stretch it into a triple in an exhibition game? It was one of those slow motion moments. Everything slowed right down while the game was going full tilt. I picked up some speed thinking this is part of the event. The third baseman was smiling and seemingly disinterested. The coach hollered to slide. Again I thought, are you nuts? It's a nothing game.

In a regular game I would slide feet first because of the way the third baseman was playing. However I thought that would be too aggressive for this event. So in a split second, I decided to ease up a bit and do a face-first "Pete Rose slide" with my hand getting to the bag first to avoid contact and possible injury to the innocent third baseman.

The throw was dead on the money and the previously casual third baseman made a great catch and covered the base, planting his left knee towards the outside part of the bag to purposely initiate contact. Well that he did. But he didn't even bother tagging me because I was safe by a foot and a half but he nailed his knee into the side of my leg between my left knee and hip.

He looked down at me and said "Nice slide. Thanks for taking it easy on me . . . . I play for real!" He laughed knowing he had purposely hurt me. I got up and finished the inning and all I could think of was the pain in my leg. Believe it or not, I had a bruise for about six years and my hip has never felt the same.

Years later, I had back surgery and the surgeon asked: "What happened here?" pointing to the now small and reddish bump on the side of my thigh. I replied: "It's a reminder to go hard all the time when the game is on".

That incident taught me to never go easy when dealing in business. Be prepared even though meetings are sometimes described as easy going. If you take the approach that today is just another ordinary day, that is likely the day when an unforeseen calamity will occur.

Know when to take a break
Remembering the right stuff, the right amount, and the right time, you will never practice when it is game time. When the work or issue is important, you will stay focused and give your best shot.

But when it is time to take a break, make sure that you also apply the peak performance principle. Equally important is to know when to turn it off. Take some time to refuel and re-energize. Use this time not only to prepare for game time but to explore other interests that you may have so that you create time for a change of pace.

Listen to other Champions
Surround yourself with true champions. If you are around people who work hard and are successful, it will be easier for you to do the same.

Champions are always encouraging others. Their passion is felt when they enter the room. Choose an inner circle of champions whose habits you admire. Listen to how they think like champions and learn from their intent, their enthusiasm, their behaviours and their routines.

It is not necessary to travel alone. Be sure to develop your network of like-minded people, so that when times are difficult, you always have somebody to assist or advise in a way that sustains and maintains your ability to think like a champion.

The above concepts and actions are the guides that keep me on the path to thinking like a champion. Respecting those and taking action at the right time ensures a consistent approach to a championship mentality. It is my secret to ensure a successful life.

ΛΛΛΛΛΛΛΛΛΛΛΛΛΛΛΛΛΛΛΛΛΛΛΛΛΛΛΛΛΛΛΛΛΛΛΛΛΛΛ

Concluding Remarks *(Ray)*

We have shared a number of points of view and ideas on how to think like a champion, a key element to be a successful leader. It takes work and effort. But then, when does success come before work? The answer is, "Only in the dictionary".

As with any of the other discussions, thinking like a champion (having a championship mentality) requires focus and concentration. Focus requires a clear and compelling vision of your desired future; concentration enables you to maintain that focus no matter what distraction happens on the road to the goal.

Watch Olympic athletes. Listen to what they say about mental preparation. When they are asked about the key to their success, they usually reply, "It's all mental". In the end, your success in any action starts and ends with your mental attitude, the ability to think like a champion.

Once in a while, leaders get bogged down in details and forget that "monkey see, monkey do". They

> *Your attitude, more than your aptitude, determines your altitude.*

take a break on the side of the road to the goal. They forget that "their attitude, more than their aptitude determines their altitude". Since they occupy the lead post, everyone in the organization follows their example. Everyone!

That happens when the thinking drifts away from an attitude of champion and the team gets distracted from the common goal. Usually, the results follow and most team members are disappointed by the inability of the team to produce to its maximum capability.

As a leader, do you want to build a winning organization or team? If that is your goal, remember the ten key elements that make thinking like a champion so effective:

- Create a vision of the desired future, with sustained commitment to it, shared with your team to inspire them;
- Sacrifice for the cause; be ready to do what you ask the team to do;
- Take no breaks; be relentless;
- Trust your team to get it done;
- Recruit winners; get people with the right attitude;
- Pay attention to details; it's the little things that kill you;

- Give people responsibility and authority so that you may hold them accountable;
- Remember people are people, not machines;
- Demand and expect excellence;
- Celebrate every successful step along the way.

It is likely the best way to enable your team to reach a higher level of excellence.

The more you activate and externalize the way you think as a champion, the more you will influence your team to follow you wherever you want to lead them. Soon, you will notice the **PULL**[37] as your team responds and aligns to the common goal, becoming a relentless and unstoppable force.

As Bruno mentioned, it takes passion to be a true champion. Some days, the fire of your passion will weaken because it's a lonely place at the top as the leader. You will find that perhaps the hardest thing to do will be to remain passionate about your role. That's when you will want to remember how to deal with being "alone at the top".

Read on as we give you some insight into the subject.

---

[37] See page 20 for definition of the term.

10 - Alone at the Top

(staying energized, creating a support system)

> *"All alone! Whether you like it or not,*
> *alone is something you'll be quite a lot."*
> **- Dr Seuss**

(Ray setting the stage)

A person in a position of leadership for a team or organization is surrounded by many people, especially his or her direct team of workers or players. It is supposedly a place full of people, complete with people interactions, and few lonely moments.

There is an unspoken reality for any leader who is committed to creating a productive and supportive environment for his or her team. At times, being the leader means " . . . alone is something you'll be quite a lot".

For a leader, many situations must be kept to oneself, dealt with personally and kept within the inner circle of the team. That often leads to being alone at the top.

From the outside, you might say that leaders should seek assistance or support and would be foolish to keep everything to themselves. I like to use the concept of the team **BUBBLE**[38]. What is inside stays inside, and what is outside stays outside.

Let me explain. It's about chemistry, and it's about confidentiality and in the end, it is

> *It's about chemistry, and it's about confidentiality and ultimately, it's about exclusivity.*

about **EXCLUSIVITY**[39]. Just think of your own experience. You don't need to have been a team leader to recognize the value of the bubble argument and the need for exclusivity. Some things are exclusive to the team. No one outside should know about or be involved in the inner workings. Only those involved in the product or service delivery really know and understand the context.

There are so many dynamics involved in human interactions inside a team bubble. People who work or play together experience so many different types of exchanges. With time, people who succeed learn to understand and accept each other unconditionally. It is a MUST if the people involved are to support, assist, back up, and accept each other for every play or every minute they work together. But to the outside world it also means "exclusivity". What is inside stays inside.

---

[38] I introduced the term "bubble" in my coaching work a few years back. It is used to represent the closed nature of a high performing team. The concept ensures that outside distractions are minimized. It also protects the team dynamics which are mission-critical for sustained success.

[39] Along with the bubble, I introduced the word "exclusivity" in my coaching sessions to consolidate all the qualities encompassed in the sense of exclusive, belonging to the people who are familiar and close to a situation. In the team context, that concept is sometime disregarded and team members put their team in peril by sharing information that should be kept confidential. Respecting exclusivity ensures that what belongs to the team process stays within the team bubble.

The leader is a key element in that "exclusivity circle". The team members trust him with personal issues and often, people who are at odds rely on him to act as an arbitrator. Of course, the team looks to the leader to protect them from the untimely or ill-advised decisions of upper management.

At times, only the leader or coach really understands what is going on. Upper management may get involved when situations would be better left to the leader to handle. At times, the leader has to defend his position without being able to reveal the real reason to the team for fear of unleashing unwanted reactions that address issues out of their control. Maintaining team chemistry requires a very delicate balancing act which is often misunderstood by upper management.

The end result leaves the leader standing alone, with no one to confide in, no one to consult for fear that the confidentiality might be broken, or that the individual team member's trust (the situation under scrutiny) is not held in respect.

Leadership can be a very lonely place, with great responsibility and not much support. That calls for the leader to be creative, aware and ready to find support whereby the team chemistry will not be jeopardized. In those moments, it is important to work to avoid being alone at the top.

The common sense solution points to friends or professional help outside the circle. Here you can have a fellow leader or coach in another field of work or play who has the same challenges in his or her team. That's where networking really pays off, first by getting to know people in the same kind of leadership position. Coaching or leadership associations are a good starting point.

A second source of support and shared knowledge is to find a personal coach, a person who is a professional in his or her field, who guarantees confidentiality, non-interference, and generates good questions to raise awareness, and stimulate creative thinking.

A third place to search for support is a good book store where you can find the writings of authors such as Jim Clemmer, Marshall Goldsmith, Ken Blanchard, Warren Bennis, Patrick Lencioni, Peter Drucker, Stephen Covey, Jack Canfield and so many others who have surveyed the field of leadership.

These authors have provided us with sound and profound reflection on the subject of standing at the front of the pack and showing the way. In some cases, it might be the best source since you can choose whatever concepts or ideas you will consider in your efforts to equip yourself to meet the challenge of being alone at the top.

Take time to gain insight into who you are. After all, your inclination toward leadership is founded on aptitudes which are already a part of your acquired skills and knowledge. Bottom line, you have them. Get good at using them!

It is necessary for you as a leader to make sure you are not alone, that you have a backup system which provides a mental and emotional resting place.

It is a lonely place at the top. Avoid falling into the loneliness trap. Make sure you have support and confidential backing to help you face the challenge. Develop a support system. Take steps to be ready when the pressure of exclusivity or confidentiality starts rising. Have an outlet valve to lighten the emotional load. Create your network, find your professional ally, believe in yourself, and stand tall in moments when you are alone at the top.

In search of ideas on how to avoid the "alone at the top" trap, let's read the reflections of our two co-authors as lonely leaders.

^^^

The Sports Perspective *(Marcel)*

We spend much time and energy figuring out ways to achieve our goals. Countless hours are spent in developing strategy, visualizing goals and preparing for our ascent to the top. Then we finally arrive, only to realize that we find ourselves alone without a plan that will ensure we can be comfortable and remain there.

Most leaders do spend time thinking about the type of things they would like to do differently from their predecessors. They think about the type of leader they would like to be, but that never really prepares one for the realities of being alone at the top.

Even if every situation is somewhat different, there are some basic principles and realities that transcend every leadership position in order to avoid being alone at the top.

When you are the leader, the realities of your situation demand that you have an awareness of your environment. In order to keep moving forward confidently, a leader must be strategic in building alliances. Furthermore, it is critical that systems and processes be put in place to ensure continuous progress toward the chosen goal. Throughout these activities, the leader should have a support system that minimizes the impact of everyday stresses.

Realities to Keep in Mind
Being a leader not only demands that you show the way but it also requires that you be adaptable and ready to face the external challenges of the position.

This may be your first time in a position of leadership or you may have been in this type of role for some time, occupying the leadership throne. Regardless, be aware that there are people around you who may wish to dethrone you. Whether it is someone who was passed over in your selection as leader, or just a very competitive driven person that works alongside of you, the challenge will be real.

Have you ever watched a nature show that follows a lion's pride? It is not long before you see a rival male try to take over the pride. There usually is a battle for leadership. Sometimes the incumbent male lion maintains his status as leader and other times it is taken over by the young rival. As experienced leaders, we have probably felt that push at work some days.

Another area that will bring different challenges is working relationships. Friends and coworkers will now interact differently with you. There will be a natural distancing that will occur. The invitations to lunch may become less frequent.

It is nothing overt, but it comes with the position. Naturally, you will begin to feel alone at the top. The social network and support systems are now reduced, but there are some basic actions that can assist you in the seat alone at the top.

Alliances

First things first! When I discuss alliances, by no way am I relating to the type of thing you see on an episode of Survivor. I am referring to building the relationships that are necessary to ensure some level of cooperation and collaboration. We want to have our efforts supported by staff and players that believe they are a part of the organization. Not everyone has to be best friends, but we have to have some level of respect and genuine interest in each other if we want to be successful.

As a leader, we have to build alliances above and below us in the hierarchy of our organization. Some are very natural because you genuinely like other people in the workplace and connect with them easily. Other relationships have to be cultivated in order to ensure integration with the total organization.

I usually separate alliances into two categories, internal and external. Both types are necessary to our success in sports, but in different ways. The internal relationships are critical for our productivity. Our external relationships are critical to our longevity and to apply the pressures that help drive us. They are important in providing a read on the perception of our organization at large. In both areas, there are people we need to lock in as allies.

As a head coach in football, some internal relationships were critical to our success. How I interacted with players, assistant coaches, support staff and management propelled us to success or acted to defeat our purpose. We had cohesion or dislocation.

On the outside, the external relationships with the fan base, media, sponsors and the league office helped to create a winning atmosphere or emphasized the challenges created by defeats on the field.

In all cases, the key is to create alliances that help you maintain your leadership position. Conversely, when an alliance impedes your effective leadership, you have to be focused enough to reduce its importance or terminate it.

Create a Support Group
The support group relates directly to the execution of your business operations plan. As a coach, your leadership group of team captains is crucial to your success. This group, consisting of team leaders, represents the groups that are most responsible for the production and execution of your team's tasks. It is important to have every key area of the team represented in the group. That means starters, back-ups, younger players and the more experienced ones.

The leaders on your team are responsible for transferring messages to their respective areas after they have understood the directives. They echo the message and continually share the vision. To have a successful relationship with any leadership group, it is necessary to meet weekly and discuss any and all potential issues from both perspectives, the leader's and the team's. It empowers your people to feel part of the process and provides them with real time and accurate information to make judicious choices when it comes to behaviour inside and outside the team confines.

For example, the usefulness of a captains' group was demonstrated when they collectively recommended the dismissal of a player because he was speaking negatively about our organization and players. I was well-served by listening to them and taking the appropriate action. That result would never have happened if we did not have that leadership process in place to build confidence and trust in their point of view.

Fostering Succession Planning
Develop other leaders that can replace you. As you create relationships in your management group, try to find people who have the potential to develop into true leaders. Spend time to find out about their aspirations. Help them to meet their goals. They will support you and be invested completely into the team goals.

It has always been gratifying to me when our assistant coaches go on to become head coaches. It certainly happened because of their merits, but I believe I made a contribution to their advancement.

Relationship to Upper Management

How you can relate with upper management is an important element in minimizing the impact of being alone at the top. Having a good working relationship that allows you to grow and have their support when things are not going well is a key to career longevity.

As long as you have influence in the management structure, you will enhance your opportunities to be successful. When that influence loses its strength or disappears, it is time to look elsewhere for another leadership opportunity.

Staying on Message with the External World

How we deal with the external forces and alliances can be critical to our working environment. We cater to the customer or in my case, the fan base, who are ultimately the most important group. These relationships are not one-on-one relationships.

In football, relationships are established through the media and the product we put on the field. In business, it may be through products or distributors. However it happens, it is important to align with the ones with whom we come face to face. In football we have a saying regarding the media, "When you lose, they cannot help you. And when you win, you do not need them." The reality is that an alliance with anyone who can promote and transfer your message on the outside is going to be important at all times.

The Importance of a Confidant

Do you have a confidant? It is important to find someone who will be brutally honest with you. Even if it means them telling you that you are not being perceived well in your organization. Nobody wants to tell the boss the truth. If you find someone that is willing to do that, it can be an enormous help in staying at the top.

Once I had an assistant coach tell me that the message I sent to the team was poorly organized and lacked a specific focus. He supported it with some of my quotes. It forced me to go back to the process, re-examine my message and make an adjustment at the next meeting. His feedback on clarification of my message helped to solidify my directives to the team.

Bottom Line
Regardless of the alliances you create internally or externally, it is important to remember one last item. Keep your friends close and keep your enemies closer.

One does not always choose his co-workers. That is the reality of the workforce in sport or business. Maintain your integrity in everything you do. Doing things for the wrong reason is detrimental to our character and integrity. However, be aware of what is transpiring around you. Not just for self-preservation, but for the good of everyone. Interact with everyone and take nothing for granted.

Spend time to really understand what is happening behind the scenes. And be ready to act in line with your values and beliefs. Stay well-connected with your team so that you are never quite alone at the top.

Beware of Creating Isolation

"Alone at the top". What fun is that! I have had to ask myself that exact question a few times. As leaders we sometimes take ourselves too seriously.

I think of the movie "Conan the Barbarian". At the end he finally reaches the top. He is sitting on his throne with his crown and a severe "I hate the world look". He is alone and has this look of "what do I do next?"

It is important to guard ourselves against this moment.

Take time to put yourself and what you do in perspective. Others have come before you and others will follow you. Try to enjoy some moments of levity. You are only one part of the whole picture. Remember who you are! And how you have become the leader!

Talk to other leaders. Have people you can speak to outside of your organization. Be careful not to take advice from them on making decisions. They are probably not qualified, just as you are not qualified to make decisions in their business. What they have in common with you is the experience of being a leader.

Often, someone may have been through what you have been through. Make sure to listen, and ask questions. Best practices are not the figment of someone's imagination. There is real living in them. Be astute. Be clear on your goals. Look to get better every day. If you work to keep connected and stay away from isolation, you will never be alone at the top.

Enjoy the ride. You never know what comes next!

^^^^^^^^^^^^^^^^^^^^^^^^^^^^^^^^^^^^^^

The Business Lens *(Bruno)*

It all starts with a thought. Then, the thought becomes a dream that it would be nice to accomplish something. You surround yourself with people that contribute. You start the journey and the next breath you take, it is over! When you reach your long term goal, you find that you are the only one there, alone at the top!

The truth of the matter is that an extremely small percentage of the people who think they want to start something actually follow through to the end. The road to the top is full of barriers and challenges. It takes determination, persistence and courage to get there.

I once worked with a fellow in a large firm. He warned me that they never learned the new person's name for at least four months because it was such a tough place to work in. You needed to be there for the right reasons if you were to survive even a few months. Those who aimed at making money in a short time were chewed out by the machine. At first, I thought the guy was trying to be funny. I saw so many come and go that, even if I tried, I could not keep track of their names. The top was definitely a hard place to reach.

My Way to the Top
In the business I am now in, I have reached the top. I am the head honcho. I run my own company. Many have

approached me throughout the years and said that they want to do what I do.

First, I thank them for considering my trade of choice and then ask them, "What do you think I had to do to get to the top?"In most cases, they randomly list the tangibles or what I call the *"Can Dos"*.

"Can Dos" are basically technical competencies that are required to get the job done. For example, developing software, repairing automobiles, typing, writing documents, etc. are *Can Dos*. They normally require technical training. Those are actions that allow stepping up the ladder to the top.

I then ask them how good they think I am at these "**Can Do**" things. They mostly respond very good or excellent. I then ask how important they think these *"Can Dos"* are on the path to the top. Most truly believe that they are the most important things or actions. That is the reason why people attend University and College, get degrees, get more degrees, get certifications etc.

Don't get me wrong, these things are very important in your journey to the top because you need to know the technical part of your business.

The big difference to be truly successful in reaching the top are the *"Want to Dos"*.

"Want to Dos" are the driving force behind why you do things. That is where passion resides. They characterize how badly you want to achieve your goal. I explain to people that unless they want to do this more than anything else in the world, someone else is willing to and will do it better.

Preparing for the attainment of the goal of reaching the top of your industry is an important step in your initial planning. It is just as important as what tools you will be using, what methodologies you will follow, the type of services you will be providing etc. If you plan and execute all of the little things that align to your goal, you will get there. The question is, "What will you do when you get to the top?"

This is more difficult than one may think. The reality is that you have never really reached the top. As we are in a changing world, you have to be a continuous learner if you are to stay at or close to the top. As Woody Hayes once said, "You're either getting better, or you're getting worst". Being at the top is a lonesome place because only you can act to maintain the position.

Consider that when you started your march to the top, you were surrounded by people and ideas that are since long gone. Make sure to take some breathing time during your ascension to the top. As obsessed as you will tend to be, it is important to *stop, breathe and re-focus*.

During this time of reflection, visualize what the end of the journey looks like. How will you feel the day after you achieve your goal of being at the top? What will you do to better your last score?

I remember a time that we were invited to bid on a large project and we were by far the smallest company to bid. It was evident that we were the token group in the mix to make the process seem valid and fair.

I worked nonstop on this proposal for four months. This included presentations, discussions and demonstrations. All of this was done while operating the business and servicing my other great clients. I spent every spare moment on this project. I really thought we had a shot at it and we eventually won the contract.

That was great news for our firm. The night we were awarded the project, I listened to Christmas music while driving home. "Christmas!!" Even though I was aware of dates and times, I had forgotten about the rest of the world. I then started thinking about who else I had neglected such as family, friends and colleagues.

Although I was on top of the world when I got in the car, moments later I thought of the fact that I was alone in this victory and nobody else really cared that I had achieved it. Being at the top was indeed a lonely place!

On your way to the top, it is important to view the process as a set of activities that are balanced with life. Life goes on with or without you. The people who are around you will move towards their goals all the same. Strive to integrate your life plans with those of the people close to you, so that the trip is not as lonely. Then you can share the rewards in the moment of success.

Recognize Those Who Help You
Another perspective to remember is that things don't always turn out the way they might have appeared at first.

We all remember the most popular kids in school. Perfect hair, perfect smile, perfect marks . . . just perfect. Sure shot winner in life. Then comes the dreaded high school reunion. Mr. or Ms. Perfect has no hair, no teeth and lost his/her fortune in a card game. Only to find out later that the kid that always sat in the back corner of the class doodling in his notebook, pretending he was not listening is now a famous and successful multi-millionaire film producer or such.

Make sure to acknowledge everyone who you meet and who helps you succeed. Without their support and sometimes challenges, you might never have reached the top.

Furthermore, one of these people may end up being your only friend when you grow old and grey. It is a good recipe to ensure that being at the top is a little less lonely.

Along the path to success in leadership, remember to share your knowledge and wisdom. Giving to others is another way to reduce the burden of being alone at the top. It allows you to gain the satisfaction of seeing others overcome the obstacles on their way to the top. In time, it may very well produce those very valuable friends that will accompany you as you travel the roads of leadership. Conversely, make sure you listen to the words of wisdom shared by others who travel in the same direction. It can be another source of support while you are alone at the top.

Leadership is an action intricately woven in the multitude of processes in our lives. The quality of that process and the resulting achievement you have savoured when you have reached the top depend on the people around you.

Recognize their contribution. Be thankful that you had the privilege of sharing knowledge and skills with them on the way to your goals. Inevitably, they will somehow help you face the challenges of being alone at the top.

Life is beautiful if you learn how to be alone at the top!

∧∧∧∧∧∧∧∧∧∧∧∧∧∧∧∧∧∧∧∧∧∧∧∧∧∧∧∧∧∧∧∧∧∧∧∧

Concluding Remarks *(Ray)*

This is one of the scariest aspects of being a leader. A person longs to reach a leadership responsibility level, and then all of a sudden, finds himself or herself all alone! Everything seems to happen in a way that creates isolation for the leader. You are a confidant, a guide, an expert, a decision maker. You may be expected to be everything to everyone, with little support to take on those challenges!

Don't be dismayed. Those challenges come with the territory. The important thing is to consider them as part of the responsibilities associated with being a leader. It is what it is. You wanted to lead? Now you have to carry that load as part of your role.

Fortunately, if you are determined to do a good job, there is a way to succeed at it, and that is called planning. It starts with being aware that, as a leader, you are "alone at the top". It is a reason for you to start recognizing the other elements of leadership we have discussed so that you end up quite comfortable "alone at the top".

We are stating the obvious but, remember that you are not alone occupying such a position. Every organization or team in every type of domain that relies on a team approach is populated by leaders who experience the same challenges as you do. As for any other aspect of leadership, step back and look at your situation objectively. Don't try to be a hero. Search for and apply best practices. The fact that you are called upon to act as a leader means that someone at one point in time concluded that you have what it takes to lead a team of your peers.

We have underlined things to remember; we have made suggestions as to how to backfill the void of "alone at the top"; we even have suggested sources of knowledge to make you a champion at handling the situation. The key as always is to be aware. Once you develop awareness of a situation, your life experience usually provides the necessary insights to deal with it effectively.

The last words are "Trust yourself".

If you have been selected to lead, there were valid reasons why you were offered the challenge. Whatever they may be, trust that, as the saying goes in the entertainment business (my daughter is a professional voice artist and actress), "It's all good!" and you have what it takes to make it.

Take the steps to guarantee that you will continue to grow as a leader. Make sure that "alone at the top" is just another challenge for your innate leadership skills.

The Last Words on Our Discussions

Here we end our reflection on **10 Discussions for Effective Leadership**. It is based on countless hours of assessment, evaluation, planning, projecting, acting and looking back as leaders in a variety of leadership positions.

We not only have observed, learned and experienced the ups and downs of leadership, but we also have at times had the privilege of sharing our experiences with peers or protégés or even strangers who asked questions about how to succeed as a leader. We were also fortunate to help many others to find their path to leadership effectiveness by modeling the behaviour that characterizes leadership excellence.

This book is a part of our reflection on our leadership careers. As leaders, we often took the opportunity to help those who wanted to learn, share and in some way improve their skills to become more effective and efficient in playing their leadership role. Our perspective on the **10 Discussions for Effective Leadership** is that these discussions should be a reference **to be contemplated** and integrated so that you can gain awareness and become more effective and efficient leaders.

The key is to be flexible and ready to take on the challenge of constant and never-ending change. Your life will certainly take you on different paths. We hope that our discussions will help you make good choices as you face the challenges of being an effective leader.

Summary and Conclusions

We have taken a trip through the minefields of leadership in an attempt at raising your awareness of some key concepts or principles that can make or break your effort to be successful as a leader.

We have mused about the layout of the land, where we have recently been and where, by all indications, we are going. Feedback reported in a credible study does not lie. Leadership strategies require modernizing, and their practitioners need training in order to adjust to the new realities. Doing it the old way simply will not do. People are much more demanding, and what we see from clients in the merchandise retail venues is happening in the hallways of leadership. People want leadership that fits their expectations.

Common sense says that it can't be quite that way. Leaders have to be leading. BUT, and it is a massive but, we must recognize that people want to be led, but led as human beings, not as machines. Remember, people hate to be managed like things; they just want their leaders to practice leadership of people, for the people.

As Jim Clemmer so cleverly put it, "Leadership is not a position, leadership is an action." And if we invest some effort in understanding the human need to be treated as a valuable person, we will all be much better off in the end.

The **10 Discussions for Effective Leadership** are but a few of the actions that ensure successful leadership. However, be sure that once you start applying a systematic, structured and consistent process to the task, other activities that devolve to a leader will soon receive the same systematic, structured and consistent treatment.

That is how our brain works. The key is to develop uniformity, consistency and repeatability of process. Once we achieve that level of execution, leadership like any task, will become much easier to exercise.

Notwithstanding our 10 Discussions, there are many other elements to the action of leadership. It is obvious that a person wanting to sustain and maintain a strong drive to lead the team will need to re-juvenate once in a while. Don't let the tank go empty. Be sure to make re-inventing yourself a continuous process.

As you probably sensed through the reading of this book, much of your success will be achieved through effective communication; it's all about communication! This brings to mind the caveat that I always share with my executive coaching clients.

Be wary of the electronic communication age! It tends to defeat your purpose of enrolling your team and aligning it to the desired goal. Face-to-face communication is the key. Be aware of the pitfall of text messaging or emailing when it comes to creating respect and trust. Make an effort to really connect with your team members. You will reap the reward of synergy that comes directly from looking a person in the eye!

We agree that there are major challenges to achieve high levels of performance. Systems are one of the main culprits. As Tom Peters[40] once reported, "Show me a company that has problems and barely succeeds and in many instances, you will find that 85 percent of the cause of unwanted results stems from the poor systems in place. Only 15 percent is attributable to weak staff performance."

In other words, don't look at people to explain their failure to achieve success. Rather look at the systems, policies, rules and other bureaucratic barriers that prevent people from doing good work. The unfortunate reality is that leadership is either the primary source of these unproductive systems or the main reason for their durability and continued maintenance.

However, a person who exercises strong leadership will recognize system failures and will act, in cooperation with his team, to reduce if not nullify the negative impact of systems in which the workers have been imprisoned.

One of the duties of the leader is to remove barriers to performance. That will take courage and persistence. You may need to transform your approach. You can help your people to develop new and productive habits and align them to your desired common purpose – then just ask them HOW

---

[40] Peters, Thomas J. and Waterman, Robert H.Jr. In Search of Excellence. HarperCollins Publishers. New York 1982.

to do it! The secret is to have a uniform, consistent and repeatable approach to your ever-changing environment.

We leave you with those thoughts and the 10 Discussions for your consideration. You always have the choice. It is your duty to choose the best for your team. Just be sure to remember that what we have presented is based on life experience, not theoretical supposition.

For those of you aspiring to lead, take a deep breath and start right now practicing the awareness of the **10 Discussions for Effective Leadership**.

Build you knowledge and internalize it. Make sure you bring it to mind and integrate it in your thinking when you are given the privilege to participate in decision-making that calls for leadership skills. It does not matter if the outcome is not your responsibility. Do as if! Prepare! Learn! Get ready for the moment when you will be faced with the challenge of leading a team. Dream, reach and achieve.

And when the moment comes, instead of cringing in the face of the challenge, you will welcome it. It will be your opportunity to put your skills to work. You will relish the challenge because you will know that you have the awareness, the skill and competency, and the ability to execute in the moment. You will be ready to shine and show your team the way to increased performance and self-satisfaction.

We hope that, as a leader, you will understand that what you believe and value will provide the guidance for your team to exceed expectations and achieve successes that one can only dream of when execution is left to chance. Make sure to stay away from trying to be the hero. Instead, focus on **creating and** enabling heroes in your team.

In our experience, we know that if you, as a leader of a group or team, make an effort to integrate the knowledge and expertise we have shared, you will greatly increase your chances of success in the journey to leadership excellence.

Ultimately, you will enable your team members to take on more responsibility and accountability for delivering service quality or quality products. You will feel the **PULL** and, as the leader, your life will be much more interesting and rewarding.

IT IS OUR GUARANTEE!!

Acknowledgements

We are indebted to our spouses for allowing us to pursue our common dream. Without their support, the journey would certainly have been more difficult. In fact, sometimes we wonder if there would be any journey at all. Louise, Julie, Lisa, perhaps you don't realize it, but we are still kids at heart. We take a creative approach to life, and at times, we don't take ourselves too seriously because it's the surest way to make it through the obstacles that line the road in applying the process of leading.

There are many people who have contributed to this piece of work. Our parents have enabled us to build our careers through the teachings and support they provided as we grew up. Ray's parents are gone. Marcel and Bruno still benefit from parental wisdom and curiosity that raises our awareness of the realities that surround us.

To our parents and families, your real life comments did more than a lot of books in keeping the fire of ambition going, a thirst to make a difference for those we work with, play with, live with. Thank you for being there at any moment, good or bad.

A big thank you to the people whom we have had the privilege of working with day in and day out, who taught us the most. "Thank you for allowing us to exercise our leadership, our clumsy tries to be the leader, allowing us to succeed and fail on the way to excellence in leadership." Those multiple situations have in a good measure led to the production of this book. We will be eternally grateful to them for sharing their efforts, applying their personal goals, desires and ambitions to help us to successfully deliver the projects or tasks that we took the responsibility to lead.

Each of us comes from a different domain, but as you read this book, you will find that, whether it is business, sports, non-profit, high tech, low tech, health, education, administration or leisure programs, the only constants are the people. And leadership is the key ingredient to their success.

We also want to acknowledge those who have contributed to putting this book together, provided editing and shared expertise to make it a readable venture. A special thank you goes to our editors, André Vermette and Rich Watson, who painstakingly went through the book word by word to smooth out the wrinkles of our musings.

We owe the uniqueness of our book cover to Marcel's wife, Julie who applied her creativity to the design of a picture conveying the idea of narrowing focus and progressive improvement to the clarity of our vision. She skillfully integrated our thoughts into an image that conveys the shifting truth of leadership action which sometimes makes reality a hard thing to believe.

As for me, as lead author, I owe a debt of gratitude to two special people. Tom Wentz has been a friend, a mentor and a wealth of insight in helping to understand the meaning of context and content when it comes to leadership and teamwork, and the need to switch from mass production to mass customization. His unrelenting effort to help people understand that the time is now for creating a new content for the modern context plays effectively into the recognized necessity to develop leaders that enable people.

The other person is Jim Clemmer, author and friend who by his uncanny skill of reducing complex issues to simple considerations through his many books on leadership, has guided my focus and efforts to reflect on and <u>decomplexify</u> (a word I created) the subject of leadership. Over time, I have learned through him to reduce leadership effectiveness to key actions that can increase results while reducing the stress associated with the associated role and responsibilities.

Lastly, in spite of the fact that writing has not been our main focus in life up to this point, we have found a common desire to explore our perspectives about a number of qualities that good leaders share. Bottom line, that desire, spawned from years of experiencing and practicing effective leadership, has enabled us to help those who are interested in avoiding some of the pitfalls of leadership through the use of simple but fundamental principles.

It is our deepest wish that you benefit from this book as we benefitted from those who showed us how to lead.

About the Authors

Marcel Bellefeuille

Marcel is the oldest of four children born and raised in Ottawa, Ontario, Canada. His story begins in a tough but inspiring housing project. Early childhood is full of real life lessons in this area of the city. His parents set an excellent example of commitment and perseverance as they successfully raised four children in a challenging environment. Possibility thinking and living were evident in all areas of their lives from a young age.

As a young man his parents supported his development through sport and education. "I can remember taking the city bus alone in grade 3 to a school outside our district" he states. "My parents always wanted me to have the best possible opportunity to receive a good education as long as I can remember". As a young football, basketball, rugby and baseball player he received the basis of his team-oriented training.

Marcel graduated high school as an Ontario Scholar and accomplished athlete, lettering in high school sports including winning the football team's MVP award as a senior at Ridgemont High School. He went on to study and play football at the University of Ottawa. He graduated with a Bachelor of Arts degree, concentration History, minor Geography. His first taste of coaching would come as a player-coach in London, England as a member of the Crawley Raiders. Through unforeseen circumstances he would finish the season as Head Coach and player.

This love of coaching would start inconspicuously as a high school coach in Ottawa. He would complete his high school football career with championships as a player and coach.

This success began to spawn even greater dreams and aspirations as a football coach. In 1994, he began coaching college football at his Alma mater, the University of Ottawa. In 1998, he took over as Head Coach and through his leadership, developed a championship team.

In 2000, in his third year as the head coach, the team won the Vanier Cup, emblematic of the Canadian Inter-university Football national championship. That turned out to be a fitting way to end his collegiate coaching career and begin the process of becoming a professional coach.

Bellefeuille has since coached 11 seasons as a professional football coach in the Canadian Football League (CFL). During that time, he held the position of offensive coordinator with both the Saskatchewan Roughriders and the Montreal Alouettes, providing him with the experience and growth opportunities that prepared him to be the head coach of the Hamilton Tiger Cats of the CFL.

Throughout his career, he has had the opportunity to coach in various roles in the Grey Cup game, conference championships and divisional playoff games.

Marcel is not only a professional football coach. He is also a polished speaker who has delivered numerous keynotes, conferences and training sessions for the benefit of many different groups. He has enjoyed teaching people of all genres on the concepts surrounding leadership, teamwork and motivation. He has made presentations to a number of private companies such as Pepsi-Cola (Gatorade), GM Canada, Nortel, Foot Locker, and also to many educational institutions.

The Coach has a heart for helping others. As he often says "I like to pay it forward. Many people have invested into my life and I would not be where I am today without them."

He is a devoted family man. Marcel takes pleasure in stating that "My wife and children are the pride and joy in my life." He is married to Julie and has four children, Ymilie, Alexandra, Mathias, and Cedrik. Just like his parents, he has worked to create an environment in which his family can grow and prosper.

Just prior to the 2000 football season, The Coach accepted Jesus Christ as his saviour. He states that this experience and subsequent journey has been the single most important event in his life. "My life was void of meaning and understanding until I accepted Jesus as my saviour."

This has provided another dimension to his coaching and teaching. The human side of being a coach has become predominant in all his interactions. Those who have had the privilege of working with him or being coached by him have experienced his comprehension and compassion.

For Marcel, it's all about being a person with integrity who respects the value of other human beings.

Bruno Lindia

 Bruno Lindia was born in Ottawa, Ontario, Canada, from a good Italian family and raised in the Preston Street area. He is the second oldest child sharing the house with father Emilio, mother Lisetta, sisters Franca and Patricia and his younger brother Vic. It was a no-nonsense household where respect of the immediate and extended family was expected. For those who know the Ottawa story, you will understand how Bruno learned early and fast about leadership and collaboration.

The neighbourhood was primarily comprised of immigrant Italian and Canadian families. This made for interesting relationship dynamics.

Attending French schools throughout his primary and secondary education years, (St-Gerard, Monseigneur Lemieux, St-Francois and École Secondaire Champlain) he learned to be socially tolerant at all levels. Language became not only a challenge but a game.

10 Discussions for Effective Leadership

While attending St-Gerard Primary School, there was a three year period in which Nuns were the main teachers. Respect and proper behavior became rule number one.

Church and spirituality were encouraged as a daily way of life. It became an absolute joy to attend Sunday mass with all of his friends. St-Gerard church, in its simplicity and humble setting was a magical place. For those who were part of a small parish, they remember it that way too. It was very cool to be an altar boy and to sing in the choir. There was a baseball diamond just outside and that is where the love of that sport began for Bruno. Kids organized the games and everyone was welcomed to play. The church and convent burned down one day and that marked one of the saddest days in the community.

From day one of kindergarten, a group of boys met for the first time and have remained lifelong supporters of one another. The group keeps each other honest and respectful. This group of lifelong friends is so different in interests and opinions yet this is what has been celebrated for all these years.

During his early youth, Bruno spent most of his time working at his father's car repair shop and gas station. At the early age of seven, he was earning nickel and dime tips from customers who liked the way he squeegeed their windshields or checked the air pressure in their tires. Although he longed to be with his neighborhood friends on summer days, he knew that he was expected to work alongside his father in the family business.

Little did he know that the lessons learned at the gas station would mould lifelong leadership models and practices, even if at times, fun and games took precedence, much to his father's disapproval. The characters that would visit daily and be part of the fun were so colorful that it warrants another book to cover those stories.

His dad's attention to detail and work ethic will never be matched. To this day, he is the model of hard work, loyalty and respect. His career as a business person spans over 50 successful years. The most amazing thing is that the turnover of his employees has been non-existent. That experience is the equivalent of an MBA. Dad surely knew how to build and maintain a team.

Bruno attended and graduated from the University of Ottawa with a business degree, graduated from Algonquin College with an Auto Mechanic certificate, graduated from Southern Alberta Institute of Technology with a Petroleum Engineering Diploma, obtained his CHRP designation (Certified Human Resources Professional), along with several other financial certificates. When asked why he pursued this diverse array of courses, Bruno will answer . . ."I wanted to learn about these things". He has always been driven by Emilio's words, "You need to be a complete individual to be in business".

Bruno played saxophone in many local bands for several years. This too was an exercise in quickly melding with the artistic groups and coming together for performances as a team.

Sports have always been important to Bruno. He has coached football at the high school, collegiate level and also in a brief stint at the professional level in France. He has always been passionate about working with athletes and sports teams.

There are so many people who have inspired him. His wife Lisa is the heart of his ideas. She has always encouraged him and supported every idea he has come up with. His children, Dominic and Matteo, are his drivers and inspiration to leave behind a proud legacy that will shape their future.

After owning his own small businesses, Bruno worked at a few large companies and found that he needed to work in a more dynamic and creative environment. DMA Canada was born. (D for Dominic, M for Matteo (his two sons) and A for our associates). As a professional recruiting company, DMA has been referred to as "the Trust-based Relationship Partner in Employee Selection Services".

Bruno also does consulting work as a leadership coach with both large and small organizations.

Raymond Perras

 Raymond Perras was born on a farm from a French Canadian family of seven children in a little town east of Sudbury, Ontario, Canada. After the passing of his mother at age eleven, his dad remarried and a half sister came to round out a family of eight.

As they lived too far from school, he was home schooled up to Grade six when bussing became available. During those early years, farm chores took up most days and schooling took place at night or on weekends. Since the oldest children were four boys, they soon played hockey on a rink put together every winter. Summer saw the kids playing ball, but football was never part of the mix until Raymond went to a private college in Cornwall in his eleventh year of schooling.

That is likely where the practice of many activities including baseball, softball, broomball, hockey, bowling, basketball, volleyball and of course football initiated a deep love of sports. There was school, and then there were sports. Being endowed with a rather strong physique, he was recruited to play fullback and linebacker for the college team.

Over five years of football, his coaches taught or confirmed his understanding of teamwork which had its roots on the farm, working with his brothers, father and grandfather. One coach in particular made a lasting impression. In the three years that Gilles Léger was at the helm, Raymond learned the values of trust, hard work, teamwork, respect, integrity, commitment and communication. Léger had an uncanny knack of nonchalantly keeping everyone focused on the common goal.

The year was 1964. It was a special year for the Cornwall College Classics (the team's name). After finishing fourth, they won a nail biter in the semi-finals, 9-8 on a last play single against Notre-Dame College, then beat the powerhouse first place team Mont St-Louis College 22-14 for the cup emblematic of the Quebec Intercollegiate Football League . To this day, Claude Mailhot, well-known sports commentator on the French network RDS, who was then playing halfback for Mont St-Louis, cannot understand how a team with only 22 healthy bodies took them down.

Looking back, Raymond lived the experience of peak performance by a whole team in those moments. Short on bodies, the team was overwhelming in its synergistic teamwork. Leadership was exemplified all the way from the head coach Léger to the players on the bench. They all knew the scheme, were committed to a common goal, and played as ONE in overcoming physical as well as mental obstacles, the first of which was a kick-off return for a touchdown by Mont St-Louis on the first play of the game.

That experience was repeated many times in sports and business over the years, confirming the importance of leadership in enabling a team to accomplish and achieve results beyond expectations. During a seventeen year career in private business and later in a five year stint with the Government of Canada, Raymond progressively learned to apply principles of leadership as a team member and as a manager.

Starting in 1982, he successfully created high performing teams that delivered projects on a timely and effective basis. In 1995, confident that he had acquired sufficient skills and knowledge to teach others, he set out in his own private company, Repars Inc., to supply coaching and training services in a number of domains including communications, project management, strategic planning, problem-solving, team building, leadership development and executive coaching.

There was no better school than helping others gain awareness of their innate abilities and coaching them to achieve greater heights of excellence. Believing in continuous learning, and focused on providing leading edge service to his clients, his efforts have been targeted at becoming certified as an instructor/facilitator, a life coach, a professional coach and a NeuroLinguistic Programming practitioner.

Since 1992, he has focused on mental preparation for athletes and coaching for coaches and business executives. The overarching theme has been leadership and the skills that allow a leader to empower and enable his team to perform at the highest possible level. Teams and business leaders have been provided with a series of techniques and processes to increase performance while reducing effort.

In October 2011, he published his first book based on the process to implement peak performance for anyone who faces challenges in the daily routine, both in business and in sports. *AiM for Life Mastery* (available on Amazon.com) is a handbook that provides a person with the insights necessary to gain awareness of personal abilities and skills, and a process to develop mastery of thinking and emotions in a way that supports peak performance. The book is intended for any person who seeks to exceed expectations in his or her daily life.

In this current endeavour, he has partnered with Marcel Bellefeuille and Bruno Lindia to produce a second book that provides the reader with some simple principles to ensure productive and effective leadership as a person responsible for a team or organization.

As for his first book, the goal is to enable the reader to achieve effort-less effectiveness in leading a team to results that are beyond expectations.

On a personal note, Raymond wishes that you cultivate a bold attitude which reflects the saying, "Shoot for the moon, if you miss, you'll be a star!"

You are encouraged to seek peak performance in all you do (**the right stuff, in the right amount, at the right time™**), and minor details will flow naturally. When excellence is your framework for success, you most likely will achieve results beyond your wildest expectations.

Currently, Raymond lives in Ottawa, Ontario and provides coaching and facilitation services to clients in both Canada and the USA. He is the proud father of three adult children, France, Serge and Joëlle who all have flourished in their respective professions. His life partner Louise is also involved as a trainer and organizational development expert. Over the years, her insight has provided many moments of re-think on the way to creating a uniform, consistent and reliable approach to leadership.

In the near future, he plans to publish a companion book to *AïM for Life Mastery*. The purpose will be to provide insight for the leader who wants to create a peak performance environment. Such an environment is the necessary context to create effort-less effectiveness, the foundation where peak performers are enabled to achieve maximum results with minimum effort.

Contact Details

To contact the authors to discuss the concepts of this book or to request help with your efforts to be a more effective leader, we can be reached at:

Raymond Perras, Peak Performance Coach:
Email: coachP@aimforlifemastery.com
Website: www.aimforlifemastery.com

Marcel Bellefeuille, Professional Sports Coach:
Email: coachmbellefeuille@gmail.com
Website: www.coachmb.com

Bruno Lindia, CHRP, DMA Canada Ltd.:
Email: blindia@dmacanada.net

About the Book

Modern organizations need effective leaders.
It is no longer sufficient to have the most advanced technology or systems to achieve maximum performance. There is growing evidence that future gains in productivity will only come from the people that do the work. Accordingly, the emphasis must now be on the human potential and not the hardware and systems.

Extensive research by the Zenger-Folkman Group has produced very sobering results showing that organizations that are exceeding expectations and beating competition have a very definite focus on developing their leadership skills and abilities.

They enable and empower their workforce to act with initiative, commitment to the goals and harmony in the group. Zenger-Folkman found that organizations that foster effective leadership increased some results over less successful ventures as follows:
- reduced turnover by 50%
- 3-5 times higher profits
- 2-3 times higher employee engagement
- 150% increased customer satisfaction
- 4-5 times more employees willing to go the extra mile.

Clearly, effective leadership is the key to superior performance at this time.

10 Discussions for Effective Leadership

In the **10 Discussions for Effective Leadership**, the authors share their experience on ten activities that can make or break a leader. By doing the right thing, practicing empowerment, trusting your team, telling the truth, planning jointly, defining your vision and sharing it, leading by example, asking good questions, thinking like a champion, and remembering that your are "alone at the top", you can ensure that you will be an effective leader.

This book aims at providing a no nonsense discussion of activities that make a big difference for leaders seeking to increase their effectiveness and exceed their expectations. It calls for "contemplation" of ways and means to transform the context and content of their leadership activities in order to enable their teams to dramatically improve their results.